W9-BXO-839

THE PRESIDENCY IN AMERICAN POLITICS

THE PRESIDENCY
IN
AMERICAN
POLITICS

EDITED BY

PAUL BRACE

Department of Politics
New York University

CHRISTINE B. HARRINGTON

Department of Politics
New York University

GARY KING

Department of Government
Harvard University

89-1189

NEW YORK UNIVERSITY PRESS
New York and London

Copyright © 1989 by New York University
All rights reserved
Manufactured in the United States of America

Library of Congress Cataloging-in-Publication Data

The Presidency in American politics / edited by Paul Brace, Christine
B. Harrington, Gary King.
p.   cm.
Bibliography: p.
Includes index.
ISBN 0-8147-1109-X
I. Presidents—United States.   I. Brace, Paul, 1954–
II. Harrington, Christine B.   III. King, Gary.
JK516.P6396   1989

353.03'7—dc19

88-37118
CIP

New York University Press books are
printed on acid-free paper, and their binding
materials are chosen for strength and durability.

IN HONOR OF OUR COLLEAGUE

Louis W. Koenig

CONTENTS

FOREWORD

The modern American presidency is at once the most visible and most hidden of our political institutions. On any given day, *what* the president of the United States is doing is known almost instantly throughout the nation, indeed, throughout the world. But *why* he and his colleagues in the executive branch do what they do, *how* they do it, and the ways in which the public perception of their activities differ from reality are all aspects of the presidency that remain elusive.

In these essays, nine distinguished political scientists analyze the Oval Office from a variety of angles. They examine the organization of the White House staff, the president's use of the appointive power to shape the judiciary, the weight of presidential authority in our tripartite system, the changes in the process by which the parties select presidential nominees, how presidents present themselves, the impact of electoral considerations on the president's economic policy decisions, and the impulse of modern administrations to substitute highly publicized symbolic gestures for serious debate on the substance of policy.

I for several reasons welcome *The Presidency in American Politics*. As a member of Congress for twenty-two years, I served during the adminis-

[ix]

trations of six presidents—Eisenhower, Kennedy, Johnson, Nixon, Ford, and Carter—and watched them all from the other end of Pennsylvania Avenue. As a political scientist who still rejoices in the rich complexity of our governmental system, I remain eager for insights into it and the institution that has emerged as its fulcrum.

But it is also because I am president of New York University that I take delight—and pride—in this volume. With its publication, New York University carries on a tradition of excellence in the study of the American presidency. Several of these essays were first delivered as lectures on our campus as part of the University's James Phelps Stokes Lecture Series. Three gifted young members of the faculty of our Department of Politics edited the final work. In dedicating their efforts to New York University Professor Emeritus Louis Koenig, they signal the large debt owed by all students of American government, particularly of the American presidency, to this eminent and distinguished scholar-teacher who for over three decades made his academic home at Washington Square. It is appropriate that the publisher of this work is the New York University Press.

As the forty-first president of the United States has just assumed office, this is a fitting time to reflect anew on the challenges and opportunities that face him. I trust this volume will find an audience not only in college classrooms but in the Oval Office and on Capitol Hill as well.

JOHN BRADEMAS
President, New York University

PREFACE

The study of the presidency can be classified into two phases. The earliest phase concentrated on the formal laws and organizational rules of the executive branch of government. Scholars studied what the president and his subordinates were permitted to do by law. Constitutional and statutory sources of presidential power were contrasted with how incumbents of the office fulfilled or exceeded their authority. Edward S. Corwin's book, *The President: Office and Powers* (1940), best represents this tradition with its primary focus on the formal, institutional powers of the presidency.

The emergence of a second phase in presidential scholarship is marked by Richard Neustadt's book, *Presidential Power* (1960). Departing from a focus on formal rules and procedures, this book concentrates on how presidents exert influence. Neustadt observed that presidents who were not leaders would accomplish very little, despite their broad constitutional authority. His analysis, and the numerous studies that follow in this behavioral tradition, identify various manifestations of presidential behavior and seek to determine the extent and the means by which presidents and their top aides get what they want in Washington.

Most of the contemporary studies of the presidency fall within this
second type of presidential research. If we contrast recent studies of the
American presidency to Corwin's work, it is striking how fragmented the
study of political phenomena has become. In addition, it is quite clear
that the presidency has become a specialized subfield within American
politics, often speaking only to scholars whose primary interest is in
presidential power and politics. Yet perhaps because of the importance of
the office and due to the wide variety of political phenomena it embodies,
scholars who are not usually identified with "presidential studies" are now
beginning to explore the presidency from the outside as it were.

This book brings together research that takes a broader view of presidential power and politics, and in some cases goes beyond traditional
approaches to the study of political phenomena. The book, therefore,
represents a current intellectual shift within American politics, one which
challenges the traditional boundaries of presidential studies. However,
the American presidency itself presents a challenging topic for students of
American politics. The book is organized to both highlight the diversity
of approaches to studying the presidency and to demonstrate how we can
understand American politics through studies of presidential performance, leadership, and image.

We begin with *predicting presidential performance*. One might envision
the scope of topics covered in American politics and in studies of the
presidency as layers or concentric circles moving out from the core which
is of the individual actors, in this case those occupying the office, to the
relationships of the office with other institutional actors and the public.
Studies of inside the executive office have focused on presidential personality and its consequences. The president's advisers and cabinet, and their
operating styles, are also of substantial interest. Similarly, the organization
of the White House staff, and how this staff influences presidential performance, is imporant to understanding the office. Studies of the president's
relations with the federal bureaucracy have also provided extremely useful
insights into policy-making and political processes.

In part I we look inside the executive office and explore the theme of
predicting presidential performance from two angles. John Kessel's chapter, based on interviews with most of the high-level staff members in the
Carter and Reagan administrations, studies White House performance
through the de facto communications network that develops among staff
units. Sheldon Goldman, in the next chapter, explains how the American

political party system serves as a good index for predicting what kind of judicial appointments presidents make.

Part II moves from inside the White House to outside it with a focus on *presidential leadership*. As we move beyond the Oval Office, the president's interactions with Congress and political parties have been a source of substantial scholarship. When considering the president's relations with Congress, we are also led to examine public opinion as it relates to presidential approval and the performance of presidents in office. The presidency and presidential elections serve to give coherence to American political parties. Presidential elections and nominations also draw attention to the political processes that select leaders.

Steven Brams, Paul Affuso, and D. Marc Kilgour study presidential leadership by developing a formal model of presidential power. They describe the formal underpinnings of presidential leadership with regard to Congress. John Aldrich's chapter then turns to the issue of how public preferences alter who will be nominated for the presidency and how nomination procedures ultimately condition presidential power. He describes the history of political reform underlying the presidential nominating system, and argues that it is based on a clash of values between those who want a manager as president and those who want a leader who reflects their ideological preferences.

As the occupant of the White House is shaped by a range of social phenomena, discussed in the first two sections of this book, the American political agenda and the electoral environment are shaped significantly by how presidents present themselves. From the perspective of people outside the White House looking in, part III covers *presidential images in American politics*. Here, Barbara Hinckley examines how presidents present themselves to the public and create institutional expectations about the office. Nathaniel Beck identifies the impact of presidential image on electoral behavior. And finally, Bruce Miroff evaluates the influence of symbolic politics in foreign policy.

There is a history behind the ideas as well as the organization of this volume. Early in Franklin Roosevelt's first term in the White House, Edward S. Corwin delivered a week-long series of lectures on the American presidency. Corwin joined such luminaries as William Howard Taft, William O. Douglas, Charles Merriam, and numerous renowned political scientists, each of whom was invited to speak at New York University's James Phelps Stokes Distinguished Lecture Series—a tradition dating from the American Civil War. Corwin published his lectures as *The President: Office and Powers*. In successive editions, it remains in print even today as a classic study of the presidency. Several chapters in this edited volume were originally presented at the 1987 Stokes Lecture Series, which was a celebration of the fiftieth anniversary of Corwin's book.

Finally, we would like to thank Farhad Kazemi, chairman of the Department of Politics at New York University, for his valuable advice and encouragement to pursue this project. In addition, we appreciate the support provided by the James Phelps Stokes Fund and the Graduate School of Arts and Sciences at New York University.

CONTRIBUTORS

PAUL J. AFFUSO received his M.A. from Essex University and is a Ph.D. candidate at New York University. He is the former director of the Academic Computing Center at NYU's Graduate School of Business Administration and now is the Associate Dean of the Leonard N. Stern School of Business. He has consulted for the New York Civil Liberties Union and the New York City Charter Revision Commission. His fields of research interest are mathematical models of political behavior and urban politics.

JOHN H. ALDRICH is Professor of Political Science at Duke University. He received his Ph.D. from the University or Rochester. He has taught at Michigan State University and the University of Minnesota. His research interest lies in the area of American politics generally, with special interest in elections and political parties. He has authored and coauthored books including *Before the Convention* and *Change and Continuity in the 1984 Elections*. He is currently at work with his coauthor on the next installment of *Change and Continuity in Elections,* and will spend next year at the Center for Advanced Study in the Social and Behavioral

Science, hoping to complete a book on the theory of political parties. He has recently completed a term as coeditor of the *American Journal of Political Science*.

NATHANIEL BECK is Associate Professor of Political Science at the University of California in San Diego. He is the associate editor of *Political Analysis* and a member of the editorial board for the *American Journal of Political Science*. He has published articles in the *American Political Science Review, American Journal of Political Science,* and the *Journal of Politics*.

PAUL BRACE is an Assistant Professor at New York University specializing in American politics. He has published research on Congress, interest groups, political economy, and judicial politics. He is currently working on articles concerning the effects of political institutions on economic growth, methodological issues in the study of state political economy, the effects of institutional structure on judicial decision making, the institutional transformation of state legislatures, and the determinants of turnout in congressional elections. He is also preparing a book-length manuscript dealing with the politics of economic growth and decline in American states.

STEVEN J. BRAMS is Professor of Politics at New York University. He has applied game theory and social choice theory to the study of voting and elections, national security and international conflict, and the Bible and theology. He is the author or coauthor of nine books, including *The Presidential Election Game* (1978), *Approval Voting* (1983), and *Rational Politics: Decisions, Games, and Strategy* (1985).

SHELDON GOLDMAN is Professor of Political Science at the University of Massachusetts at Amherst. He is the author or coauthor of ten books, the most recent being *Judicial Conflict and Consensus* (1986), *Constitutional Law* (1987), and *American Court Systems* (1989). His articles have appeared in political science and law journals and include a series published in *Judicature* concerning federal judicial appointments.

CHRISTINE B. HARRINGTON is an Assistant Professor of Politics at New York University. She is the author of *Shadow Justice: the Ideology and Institutionalization of Alternatives to Courts* (1985) and the coeditor of the *Law and Society Review* Special Issue on *Law and Ideology*. She has published articles on dispute processing and litigation, regulatory reform, legal realism in social science research, the feminization of the legal profession, and the ideology of participation in legal forums. She is a consultant to the Ford Foundation on law and society research, and is on the editorial boards of the *Law and Society Review*, *Law and Policy*, and *Studies in Law, Society, and Politics*. Her manuscript in progress, *The Legal Construction of Politics: Legal Practice and the Administrative State*, examines the role of the legal profession in shaping the politics of the administrative state.

BARBARA HINCKLEY has taught at the University of Wisconsin, Madison, and at Cornell and is now a Professor of Politics at New York University. She has been a Guggenheim Fellow and Vice-President of the American Political Science Association and has worked as an election consultant for ABC News. Her books include *Stability and Change in Congress*, *Congressional Elections*, *Coalitions and Politics*, and *The Symbolic Presidency*.

JOHN H. KESSEL has taught at Amherst and Mount Holyoke colleges and the University of Washington. Since 1970 he has been Professor of Political Science at Ohio State University. His books include *The Goldwater Coalition*, *The Domestic Presidency*, and *Presidential Parties*. His articles have appeared in the *American Political Science Review*, *American Journal of Political Science*, *Social Science Quarterly*, and other professional journals. He has been a member of the Council of American Political Science Association, editor of the *American Journal of Political Science*, and president of the Midwest Political Science Assocation.

D. MARC KILGOUR is Professor of Mathematics at Wilfrid Laurier University in Waterloo, Canada, as well as Adjunct Professor of systems engineering at the nearby University of Waterloo. His research and consulting interests are in mathematical modeling, principally conflict modeling and game theory. With Steven J. Brams he published *Game Theory and National Security* (1988). He won the Public Choice Society's 1984 Duncan Black Award for an article written with Terrence J. Levesque on the Canadian Constitution. He has recently published papers in mathematics, political science, system engineering, operations research, philosophy, and biology journals.

GARY KING is Associate Professor of Government at Harvard University. He is a frequent contributor to scholarly journals in the areas of political methodology and American politics, author of *Unifying Political Methodology: The Likelihood Theory of Statistical Inference* (forthcoming), and coauthor of *The Elusive Executive: Discovering Statistical Patterns in the Presidency* (1988).

BRUCE MIROFF is the author of *Pragmatic Illusions: The Presidential Politics of John F. Kennedy* and of numerous articles on the presidency and political leadership. His current project is *The Tribe of The Eagle: American Images of Political Leadership*. He teaches political science at the State University of New York at Albany.

THE PRESIDENCY IN AMERICAN POLITICS

I

PREDICTING PRESIDENTIAL PERFORMANCE

ONE OF the frequently cited hallmarks of a mature science is theory that yields accurate predictions about observable phenomena. While not universally accepted, some scholars within the natural and social scientific communities have sought to make predictions about phenomena of interest within their respective fields. Directly or indirectly the goal of prediction has also influenced political science. In some areas of American politics the goal of prediction has led to impressive results. For example, scholars studying Supreme Court decision making, election outcomes, and roll calls within Congress have produced remarkably accurate predictions. Alternatively, other areas of political life have been highly resistant to prediction. Presidential performance is one such area.

The presidency is both an individual and an institution. Presidential performance, however evaluated, results from the complex interplay of individual presidents, the patterns of influence that emerge within their administrations, and the wide variety of issues they confront as well as avoid. Among the more challenging tasks in the study of the presidency is to address the variability in the conditions which influence presidential performance. To predict systematically and accurately the performance of presidents would require substantial information about those initial conditions which affect presidential decision making. In addition, of course, a theory of presidential performance must logically relate these conditions to what the executive branch does. On top of this, access to observe the critical operations within the White House is extremely limited. Thus predicting presidential performance is enigmatic yet compelling.

The two chapters in this section highlight the difficulties of developing predictive theories of presidential performance. In chapter 1, "White House Structure During Reagan's Second Term," John Kessel sheds new light on patterns of influence among the president's top advisers and White House organizational units. Kessel argues effectively that "while the presidency has some unique features to which we must give due attention, the methods of studying political behavior are just as applicable to the presidency as they are to any other political institution." He illustrates this with an important analysis of data he collected from semistructured interviews with virtually every senior member of the Reagan and Carter White Houses. On the basis of his research, he stresses the limits of our capacity to predict specific actions by administrations.

In chapter 2, "Judicial Appointments and the Presidential Agenda," Sheldon Goldman focuses on presidential performance in one important area—the appointment of Supreme Court justices and lower federal court judges. He illustrates how, at various times, presidents have used appointments to lead or to bargain. Some presidents have sought to pursue a very specific policy or ideological agenda. These presidents try to appoint justices who they expect will reflect their ideological preferences and objectives once on the bench. Whereas these presidents view the courts as integral to their administration's policy goals, other presidents have used their court appointments to build support within their political party. Presidents who pursue a partisan strategy are able to use appointments as part of a bargaining process in order to achieve other goals, rather than viewing appointments as ends in themselves. These partisan goals sometimes coincide with a president's policy goals, but the two are analytically and empirically distinct. Goldman argues that judicial appointments have been closely linked to presidential agendas, and the content of these agendas often reflects the ongoing conflicts within the American political party system. By narrowing the analysis of presidential performance to one area, Goldman suggests ways of predicting presidential behavior.

ONE

White House Structure During Reagan's Second Term

John H. Kessel

STABILITY AND CHANGE

When the New York University Press published Edward S. Corwin's *The President: Office and Powers* in 1940, there was barely a hint of the presidency as the institution exists in the 1980s. Franklin Roosevelt was doing many of the things that we have come to recognize as characteristic of the modern presidency, but few of the staff units that would allow future presidents to do these things on a regular basis existed. Roosevelt had appointed a press secretary in 1933; a White House office with half a dozen assistants had been created in 1939; the Bureau of the Budget, the predecessor of the present Office of Management and Budget (OMB), had been moved from the Treasury Department to the new Executive Office of the President at the same time. Of the institutional elements that existed in 1940, these are the only survivors.

Since that time, there has been considerable institutional development. The National Security Council (NSC) came into being during the Truman administration, and has become the principal coordinator of foreign policy on the president's behalf. A Council of Economic Advisers was created about the same time, and joined the Treasury Department and what is now OMB as a member of the troika concerned with economic policies. The Nixon administration created a Domestic Council that was supposed to coordinate domestic policy as the NSC did foreign policy. It has had a couple of name changes since, but has survived and was a major player during the Nixon and Carter administrations. Staff support for the imperative policy areas of international affairs and economics came first, but by 1970 there was a full set of agencies dealing with policy coordination.

Agencies also have been created to provide interface with groups with which the president has regular contact.[1] The press secretary's office, now joined by a communications director, provides an access point for the media. A congressional liaison office was organized by President Eisenhower to provide regular contact with Capitol Hill. And an Office of Public Liaison was set up during the Ford administration so there would be a unit whose principal responsibility was dealing with interest groups. Again, by the 1970s a set of liaison offices had been created.

There are many important questions to be asked about the presidency. One concerns its durability. At opposite poles are one interpretation that holds the presidency is so transient that it does not really exist across administrations, and another that holds that the presidency is so stable that one cannot tell any difference between one administration and its successor.

The first view was stated by James David Barber, author of *The Presidential Character:* "We really don't have a presidency. All we have is a succession of presidents" (1980). Support for this view can be found in the extent of personnel turnover. The Supreme Court changes one justice at a time. The United States Senate regards itself as a continuing body. Over 80 percent of the House members have been members of the preceding Congress.[2] Contrast what happens with the presidency. As is well known, on January 20, 1981, Ronald Reagan was sworn in to succeed Jimmy Carter. As is less well known, all Carter political appointees had to surrender their White House passes and be out of the building by 12:00 noon. Shortly after 12:00 noon, a team of Reagan appointees arrived at the White House to make preparations for the arrival of the larger party that was due after the inaugural ceremony. With total turnover of the principal decision makers, there is very little institutional memory. Another argument for lack of stability is that the working arrangements in any White House reflect a particular president's management style. For example, Howard Baker said that he talked with several of his predecessors, but discovered little of value because each White House was organized around a unique person with a unique way of doing business.

The opposite view of an unchanging presidency is suggested by the title of a paper by Joseph Pika: "Changing the Players but Not the Game" (1984). In his analysis, Pika draws on an idea of *deep structure* put forward by Hugh Heclo. This structure, Heclo writes:

> is a web of other people's expectations and needs. On the surface, the new president seems to inherit an empty house. In fact, he enters an office already shaped and crowded by other people's desires. . . . [The office is a] raw, exposed ganglion of government where immense lines of force come together in ways that no single person can control. The total effect is to program the modern president. (1981, p. 165)

This view rests on an assumption of an unchanging political environment. Regardless of who is elected, each new president has to deal with the same set of sovereign powers overseas, the same economy and domestic problems at home, the same press corps, the same Congress, and so forth.

Not only has the presidency changed since World War II, but so have the methods of studying that institution. In Corwin's interpretation, the presidency was essentially a subfield of constitutional law. One learned what the Supreme Court had held in various cases, added a few facts about the office, and that was really all one needed to know. There are some who still follow a "powers and duties" approach, but since about 1970 there has been a search for new ways to assess the institution. There is not agreement yet, but there is an active search for more powerful methods of analysis.

My own view is that while the presidency has some unique features to which we must give due attention, the methods of studying political behavior are just as applicable to the presidency as they are to any other political institution. Accordingly I do not see either of the rival interpretations about the stability of the institution as views to be defended, but as sources of hypotheses to be tested. Further, since pollsters have learned about voters through survey techniques, and legislative scholars have learned about congressmen by asking them questions, I have done the same thing in the White House.

Let me mention two examples of this. Using a series of structured questions suggested by Herbert Simon's theories of influence (Simon, Smithburg, and Thompson 1958), and drawn from Heinz Eulau's study of

Bay Area city councils (Eulau and Prewitt 1973), I inquired about the relative influence of various members of the Carter and Reagan White House staffs. Influence scores for persons holding comparable positions on the Carter and Reagan staffs are shown in table 1.1.[3] While the individual influence scores are not free-floating, there is considerable variation between the members of the Carter and the Reagan staffs. Stuart Eizenstat, Charles Schultze, Jody Powell, and Anne Wexler were much more influential on the Carter staff than were the heads of the same units on the Reagan staff. On the other hand, William Clark, Ken Duberstein, and David Stockman were more highly regarded in the Reagan White House than were their counterparts on the Carter staff. The implication of this is lack of continuity between succeeding White Houses. On this evidence it would seem that one presidency does not resemble another.

But look at White House perceptions of the units themselves, as shown in table 1.2. These were measured using questions based on some psychophysical research at the State University of New York at Stony Brook.[4] Here there is clear evidence of continuity across the two White House staffs, and evidence of an enduring hierarchy among the organizational units.

Drawing rather arbitrary lines, there are three categories. The National Security Council, the congressional liaison office, and the Office of Management and Budget are the most important. Two of the units, the Council of Economic Advisers and (in the Reagan administration) the Office of Policy Development that deals with domestic policy, might be called middleweights. The least important offices are the two outward-looking units: the press secretary's office and the Office of Public Liaison.

TABLE 1.1
Influence Scores of Carter and Reagan Unit Heads

Unit	Carter Head	Influence Score	Reagan Head	Influence Score
NSC	Brzezinski	136	Clark	268
Cong. Liaison	Moore	15	Duberstein	125
Domestic	Eizenstat	343	Harper	169
OMB	McIntyre	90	Stockman	262
Cncl. Econ. Adv.	Schultze	102	Weidenbaum	1
Press	Powell	251	Gergen	84
Pub. Liaison	Wexler	138	Dole	0

TABLE I.2
Importance Scores of Carter and Reagan Staff Units

Unit	Carter Score	Reagan Score
NSC	52.2	54.9
Cong. Liaison	47.7	47.1
Domestic	46.0	36.6
OMB	42.3	55.3
Cncl. Econ. Adv.	34.5	26.1
Press	29.9	25.8
Pub. Liaison	18.2	14.3

There were a couple of noticeable changes between the two administrations. The Domestic policy staff was a major player in the Carter administration, but not in the Reagan administration. OMB was more important in the Reagan White House than it was in the Carter White House. But these two units are the only ones that changed order in the overall hierarchy. All the other units had very similar scores in two quite different White Houses.

It turns out then that there is basis for both of the conflicting interpretations about stability. In the presidency, as indeed with political institutions, there is simultaneous stability and change. What systematic investigation does is to make it possible to learn just where the change is taking place. This, in turn, allows us to begin to develop an understanding of the presidency.

REAGAN'S SECOND ADMINISTRATION

"The Reagan administration is in terrible shape," Elizabeth Drew wrote in February 1987. "Of late, it has seemed almost clinically dysfunctional" (1987, p. 95). Nor was it necessary to turn to journalists to find statements that the Reagan administration had been mortally wounded. Dom Bonafede surveyed 161 presidential scholars that same month, and a full 30 percent responded that President Reagan had been irrevocably wounded (1987, p. 555).[5] This invites some skepticism. Through much of 1986, we were reading that President Reagan leapt tall buildings at a single bound before breakfast, and then flew out to the ranch to spend the afternoon clearing brush. It seems likely that the Reagan administration was not quite so masterful as it was said to be earlier, and was not quite so inept as it was being portrayed in early 1987.

Governments, after all, do not stop functioning. Hugh Heclo has a marvelous passage in *A Government of Strangers* in which he discusses all the things that the administration was doing on the afternoon of Richard Nixon's resignation. The Defense Department announced sixty-one new contracts. The Treasury Department was working on contingency plans to be ready for some anticipated bank defaults. The Office of Legislative Reference was responding to congressional inquiries about the president's position on some legislative proposals. The Transportation Department was finishing up work on some mass transit grants. And so forth (1977, pp. 9–10). In commenting on the impact of the Iran-Contra affair, Dean Rusk said that the State Department would be sending out something like 3,000 cables that day, just as they did every working day.

In the spring of 1987, Reagan's "third" administration was being mentioned, the reference being to Howard Baker's having replaced Donald Regan as chief of staff. No doubt any president could use Senator Baker's conciliatory skills, but before dismissing the "second" Reagan administration, it is worth taking a moment to look at its organization. In speaking of the Reagan organizational arrangements, I will not be dealing with such deep structural factors as patterns of influence and communication, but rather with the surface arrangements to transact business.

Perhaps the most important thing that Donald Regan did for the position of chief of staff was to seek the position. (You will recall that it was Regan who approached James Baker with the suggestion that they trade jobs.) When a secretary to the Treasury, whose position dates back to 1789, was willing to give up that post to become chief of staff, he confirmed the status that the White House post had achieved in all but protocol. We saw further evidence of this when Senator Baker was willing to give up his own presidential aspirations to take the chief of staff post.

After he became chief of staff, Mr. Regan became the principal channel of communication to the president. This was a considerable change from the first Reagan administration. Then there were three people—James Baker, Edwin Meese, Michael Deaver—who had walk-in privileges with the president. (The number was increased to four when William Clark became assistant to the president for national security affairs.) The three aides had a regular meeting with the president every morning at nine o'clock. In the second administration, Donald Regan had a regular meeting with the president every morning. The change from the third person plural to the third person singular suggests the real difference between the first and second administrations.

Another important difference between James Baker and Donald Regan lay in the types of appointments they made. To establish liaison with Congress and the media, James Baker selected Max Friedersdorf as assistant to the president for legislative affairs and David Gergen as communications director. In both cases, Baker was bringing people into the White House who already had experience with the Ford administration. Leaving aside the question of their individual ability (and it was genuine in both these cases), Baker's actions augmented his own political ability by bringing in people who knew how the White House worked and how Washington worked. Donald Regan also made a number of appointments when he first came over to the White House, but most of his key appointments were individuals who had worked with him before, and who knew how *he* worked. Regan did not have much feel for the folkways of Washington, and he did not appoint other people who could help him in this regard.

Donald Regan's most important change dealt with the organizational arrangements for domestic policy-making. He asked both Alfred Kingon, who was in the Treasury Department, and Roger Porter, who had worked with Regan and had been a member of both the Ford and Reagan White House staffs, to give him some ideas on policy organization. Their recommendations were rather similar. As they were put into effect, foreign and defense policy was left in the hands of the National Security Council, but the domestic policy process was channeled through an Economic Policy Council and a Domestic Policy Council.[6] These two councils had been left in place by Howard Baker when he became chief of staff, and remained as foci for decision making throughout Reagan's second term.

Both the internal White House units (OMB, for example) and the relevant cabinet departments have seats on these councils. This represents a shift from arrangements in which the cabinet departments reported to the president through a White House unit. When an undersecretary contacted the Johnson, Nixon, or Carter White House through a domestic staff member, and the same staff member called the undersecretary back to report the president's decision, the undersecretary often felt that he was at some remove from real power. Of course, all skillful White House staff members consulted at length with the departments involved in any decision so the outsiders would be confident that their views had been taken into consideration in the decision. Furthermore, the staff members were under instruction that department views were to be forwarded to the president. Even so, the growth of power of the White House staff was hard on the persons who were in the executive departments—and it does not seem accidental that a cabinet member who became chief of staff would implement a system in which department and White House personnel sat around the same table as equals.

All three councils—the National Security Council, the Economic Policy Council, and the Domestic Policy Council—were chaired by the president. The president did attend meetings, usually when a decision was about to be made. But in his absence the person who chaired the Economic Policy Council was Treasury Secretary James Baker, and the person who chaired the Domestic Policy Council was Attorney General Edwin Meese. This meant two things. First, Baker and Meese had very full plates. They not only had major departmental responsibilities, but coordination responsibilities inside the White House. Second, Baker and Meese were two of the three most important aides during the first administration. Consequently, in spite of the claim that President Reagan was not receiving such good advice as he had during his first term, much of the policy advice was coming from the same people.

Most major policy decisions went through these three councils.[7] This is evidence of an effort to keep things in proper channels, to keep things under control. If there are multiple routes into the White House, if an agency can choose whether to bring a matter to the attention of, say, the Office of Policy Development, a Council on Economic Affairs, a Council on Commerce and Trade, or to have interest group allies bring it to the attention of the Office of Public Liaison, the initiative lies with the agency that favors the proposal. They can choose the unit in which their proposal will get the most sympathetic hearing. The situation is not unlike that where a friendly Speaker of the House can refer a bill to a committee that is more sympathetic rather than less sympathetic. So a reduction of the number of venues, and a prior definition of the jurisdiction of each by the White House, gives the White House greater control.

There is an argument over which presidential function is more important: is it to make the proper decision or is it to implement the decision once it is made? If you think it is to make the proper decision, it follows that you want to structure things so the president hears the widest range of choices. If you think it is to get the agencies to follow presidential decisions that have been made, then you want to give oversight power to those who know what the president wants. One can further argue that these two functions vary in importance over a president's terms of office. When he is first sworn in, basic decisions about the administration's direction need to be made. At that stage you want to expose the president to debate over desirable courses of action. Late in an administration, most of the basic decisions have been made. At that point, you want greater control so as to defend initiatives that have been begun earlier. This was the direction in which the Reagan administration moved.

Finally, the Economic Policy Council and the Domestic Policy Council were reasonably busy. The Economic Policy Council's agenda was filled with trade items. Problems were called to the administration's attention, usually by industry complaints, and were examined, first by a trade policy staff committee, and then by a trade policy review group. If these groups found merit to the complaint, the item came before the Economic Policy Council which made a recommendation to the president. This was the process that led to the U.S.-Japan semiconductor agreement, and then to American retaliatory action when Japan broke the agreement.

One of the important items handled by the Domestic Policy Council was catastrophic illness insurance. The bill that the administration submitted came, as was reported, from Secretary Bowen at Health and Human Services. What was not given much attention was that the debate on catastrophic illness in the Domestic Policy Council extended over some fifteen months before President Reagan ultimately opted for the bill that was submitted. To return to my initial point that government does not stop, this is an example of something that began long before the Iran-Contra matter became known to the public, on which debate was going on within the administration while media and public attention was focused on that crisis, and which may lead to policy results after the Iran-Contra affair has been disposed of.

OUR ABILITY TO PREDICT

The Iran-Contra affair engulfed the Reagan presidency in late 1986 and engaged public attention for much of 1987. The gentlest interpretation was that serious mistakes had been made. One did not have to look very far to find people who said that the Iran-Contra affair destroyed the Reagan presidency in the same sense that Vietnam destroyed Johnson's,

Watergate destroyed Nixon's, and the hostage-taking in Tehran destroyed Carter's.

Political scientists who study voting are now able to predict election outcomes with reasonable accuracy. In July 1984, for example, Steven J. Rosenstone employed a statistical model to predict that Walter Mondale would receive 41.1 percent of the vote, and would carry three states plus the District of Columbia (1985). In November, Mondale received 40.8 percent of the vote, carrying only Minnesota and the District of Columbia, and received 48 and 49 percent of the vote, respectively, in Rhode Island and Massachusetts, the two other states Rosenstone had said he would carry.

Should presidency scholars have been able to make an equivalent prediction about the Iran-Contra affair? I do not think so. One reason is the nature of the event. An election is much simpler. For practical purposes, most voters have only two decisions, whether to vote or not, and whether to vote for a Republican or a Democrat. It is not accidental that great progress has been made in studying voting. But when we turn to the Iran-Contra affair itself, the Tower Commission did call it an aberration. Knowledge of any phenomenon does not allow you to predict deviant cases. A person who knew a lot about the National Security Council ought to have been able to tell you how the NSC usually handles matters, but not what they might do when they depart from customary procedures. The other reason concerns what we know about the presidency. My own slowly accumulating knowledge deals with underlying structures of the presidency. This would not permit me to forecast a particular set of events any more than knowledge of a skeleton would allow a physician to know how a body would react to a particular virus.[8]

Now, just what did we know in advance of the Iran-Contra matter? To begin with, the National Security Council was recognized as the most important presidential staff unit (p. 155).[9] One reason it was so highly regarded was the nature of its expertise. Staff members knew, for example, about nuclear throw weights, various political factions in Pakistan, and any number of arcane facts. Members of other White House units did not know about these things, and they *knew* they did not know. On domestic politics there were several staffs—congressional liaison, Office of Policy Development, and the Domestic Policy Council—that knew something about whatever subject matter was being discussed. Consequently any staff dealing with domestic politics was more likely to have its positions challenged within the White House than was the NSC (pp. 154–55).

It also happens that the National Security staff is the most isolated of all of the principal White House policy units. When communication patterns on the White House staff are analyzed one finds that while the domestic staff, legislative liaison staff, OMB, and other domestic political units are in frequent contact with each other, the NSC has less contact with other staffers than any other unit (pp. 93–98).

The Reagan administration inherited a real problem with the National Security Council, and they never solved it satisfactorily. From the Kennedy administration through the Carter administration, the National Security Council had acquired more and more power. This had progressed to the point that the national security assistant had become a real rival to the secretary of state, as was the case with Henry Kissinger and William Rogers, or with Zbigniew Brzezinski and Cyrus Vance. When the Reagan administration came into office, they deliberately reduced the role of the national security adviser to avoid this rivalry (pp. 120–21). But while they had gone through four national security assistants by the time the Iran-Contra affair became public, they never solved the problem of how to reduce the importance of the national security adviser, and at the same time have someone knowledgeable and influential enough to deal with the rival views of State, Defense, and the CIA.

In comparison with the Eisenhower, Kennedy, and Nixon administrations, the Reagan administration entered office without much foreign policy experience. Ronald Reagan was comparable to Lyndon Johnson in that most of his pre-presidential experience had concerned domestic policy. There had always been an anti-Communist component in Reagan's thinking, but his principal beliefs were a need for a reduced role for government and a reduction in taxes. His principal cabinet officers also came from backgrounds in domestic politics. Secretary Schultz was an academic economist who had held the Labor, OMB, and Treasury portfolios. Secretary Weinberger was a Harvard Law graduate who had been California Republican state chairman, state finance director, and then had headed FTC (the Federal Trade Commission), OMB, and HEW (the Department of Health, Education, and Welfare) during the Nixon administration. Furthermore, in making appointments the Reagan administration required an appointee's agreement with the president's policy positions (p. 51). The effect of this was to limit the number of potential foreign policy advisers.

Finally, according to testimony presented to congressional investigators, only two members of the NSC staff were aware of the diversion of funds. Lieutenant Colonel Oliver North ran the operation, apparently with the encouragement of CIA director William Casey. Admiral John Poindexter stated that he did not report the fund diversion to anyone else. What Admiral Poindexter did report to President Reagan was routed through Donald Regan. Whatever else may be said about these persons,[10] no one ever associated them with innovative or subtle foreign policy.

I would submit that these things taken together—a respected, isolated staff reporting to persons innocent of much expertise in foreign policy—allow us to understand that something *could* go wrong. They do not allow us to forecast that something *would* go wrong, still less to know in advance just what might happen. In short, general knowledge lends perspective to events. It allows us to understand them, but it does not—and *should* not—duplicate knowledge of the particular events themselves.

Our goal in studying the presidency ought to be general understanding. If knowledge is to be used efficiently, it needs to apply to as wide a class of events as possible. After all, at the time of writing we do not know who is going to be elected president in 1988 or just what difficulties the new administration will face. But if we are successful in our search for general knowledge about the presidency, that knowledge ought to help us understand a wide range of events if and when they do take place.

NOTES

1. The word interface may sound too modern and mechanical, but my dictionary says the word dates from 1882, and means "the place at which two independent systems meet and communicate with each other." This is what is happening with the White House liaison units.

2. This is an average figure for post–World War II Congresses. If one takes only those who run for reelection (and thus excludes those who retire for one reason or another), the average goes up to over 90 percent.

3. For further discussion of these scores and details of their construction, see my *Presidential Parties* (1984), pp. 98–108, 591–92.

4. For further discussion of these scores and details of their construction, see my *Presidential Parties* (1984), pp. 105–8, 154–56, 592–93.

5. Nearly two-thirds of those responding took the less severe view that Reagan had been seriously damaged, but not irrevocably so.

6. There had been a number of cabinet councils during the first administration, one on economic policy, one on natural resources and agriculture, and so forth. However, the two new bodies did not simply continue the economic

council, and combine the others into a single domestic council. The dividing line was a little different.

7. A bill to be submitted to Congress would be a policy decision as opposed to a decision on whether or not President Reagan would schedule a press conference. There is a whole range of decisions being made continually within the White House that have relatively little to do with policy.

8. By using the skeleton as a metaphor, I am not trying to make a claim about the importance of my findings, only to illustrate the kind of information I have. Another presidential scholar has characterized my analysis as "anatomy" (Rockman 1986, p. 121).

9. The page references from here on all refer to my *Presidential Parties* (1984). I include them simply to make the point that I thought these things were important enough to include in a book I published in 1984. They are not matters I remembered only when the Iran-Contra affair became known to the public.

10. While many negative comments were made about Donald Regan in the wake of the Iran-Contra affair and his subsequent resignation, it should be recalled that he was regarded as the best of Reagan's initial cabinet appointments. "He's a class act," and "he's the rising star" were typical early comments (*U.S. News and World Report* 1981, p. 15).

REFERENCES

Barber, James David (1980). *The Presidential Character*. Englewood Cliffs, N.J.: Prentice-Hall.

Bonafede, Dom (1987). "Spoiled Legacy." *National Journal*. (March 7) pp. 555–59.

Corwin, Edward S. (1957). *The President: Office and Powers 1787–1957: History and Analysis of Practice and Opinion*, 4th ed. New York: New York University Press.

Drew, Elizabeth (1987). "Letter from Washington." *The New Yorker*. (February 16) pp. 95–107.

Eulau, Heinz, and Kenneth Prewitt (1973). *Labyrinths of Democracy: Adaptations, Linkages, Representation, and Policies in Urban Politics*. Indianapolis: Bobbs-Merrill.

Grossman, Michael Baruch and Martha Joynt Kumar (1981). *Portraying the President: The White House and the News Media*. Baltimore: Johns Hopkins University Press.

Heclo, Hugh (1977). *A Government of Strangers*. Washington, D.C.: The Brookings Institution.

———— (1981). "The Changing Presidential Office" in Arnold J. Meltzer, ed. *Politics and the Oval Office*. San Francisco: Institute for Contemporary Studies.

Kessel, John H. (1984). *Presidential Parties*. Homewood, Ill.: Dorsey Press.

Koenig, Louis W. (1987). *The Chief Executive*, 5th ed. New York: Harcourt Brace Jovanovich.

Pika, Joseph A. (1984). "Changing the Players but Not the Game: The Organizational Presidency." A paper prepared for delivery at the annual meeting of the American Political Science Association, Washington, D.C., September 1.

Rockman, Bert (1986). *The Leadership Question*. New York: Praeger.

Rosenstone, Steven J. (1985). "Why Reagan Won." *The Brookings Review*. (Winter) pp. 25–32.

Simon, Herbert A., Donald W. Smithburg, and Victor A. Thompson (1958). *Public Administration*. New York: Knopf.

U.S. News and World Report (1981). "Rating Reagan's Cabinet." (July 27) pp. 14–20.

TWO

Judicial Appointments and the Presidential Agenda

Sheldon Goldman

During the two terms of the Reagan administration, more sustained attention was paid by the media and various public and private interest groups to the selection of federal judges to all court levels than at any time since the Roosevelt administration. This was understandable because not since the Roosevelt administration were federal judges seen as playing so central a role in the presidential domestic policy agenda.

Of course, it has long been known that judicial decisions are not brought by constitutional storks but are the result of individual judges viewing the law through their philosophical and ideological lenses.[1] This fact of legal life, however, took on a new urgency for the Reagan administration starting in the early months of the first term as it began to put in place a program of systematic philosophical and ideological screening of judicial candidates. The courts were seen as centers of policy-making activity on social issues important to the administration—abortion, prayer in the public schools, busing for the purpose of school desegregation, affirmative action at the workplace, the rights of criminal defendants, sexual privacy—and this by no means exhausts the list.

The courts were seen by the Reagan administration as being so activist in the civil rights and civil liberties spheres as to have created an imbalance in the federal system contributing to the evisceration of state powers and responsibilities and the expansion of policy-making by the federal judiciary beyond its capacity. A special White House working group on federalism, rather paradoxically, also faulted the judiciary for *not* being activist in the protection of the state's role in *economic* policy-making and for permitting Congress, in the view of the working group, to misuse its commerce power as the basis for national regulation of the economy.[2] There are some who saw as the hidden agenda of these Reaganites the restoration of the constitutional rights of corporate America as they existed before the New Deal era.

In other words, judicial appointments were seen by the Reagan Administration and observers of contemporary American politics as intimately linked to the presidential agenda in the domestic affairs arena.[3] This raises the questions of how the Reagan administration's linkage of judicial appointments to the presidential agenda compared to that of previous administrations and whether what Reagan did went beyond anything we have seen in the history of American politics.

THEORETICAL FRAMEWORK

In answering the questions raised above it is useful to make a distinction between the president's *policy agenda* and the *partisan agenda* although, to be sure, both are played against the backdrop of party politics.

The *policy agenda* refers to the substantive policy goals or objectives of an administration and includes its legislative and administration program. The *partisan agenda* refers to the use of presidential power to shore up political support for the president and for the party.

Although the policy agenda may be furthered at the same time as that of the partisan agenda, what distinguishes one from the other is the motivation behind the exercise of presidential power. If the concern is primarily to mend political fences, reward partisan supporters, provide incentives for party organizations, satisfy a constituency group within the party's coalition, or even simply to be on good terms with a senator, the actions of the president can be considered to be *partisan agenda* actions even if there are also policy consequences. If the concern is primarily to further the president's policy agenda, with partisan considerations of less concern, perhaps even to the point of the president willing to risk alienating one political ally or constituency group at the expense of another, *or* if the action has little partisan consequence, the action can be considered a *policy agenda* action. Because motivation is the central characteristic distinguishing a policy agenda from a partisan agenda action, we are dealing with political phenomena that are difficult to study systematically. That means we must rely on detailed case studies and ultimately depend upon the interpretation of the researcher in classifying presidential behavior. We should also acknowledge that there may be instances where both motives seem to be of equal importance or where it may be impossible to determine which motive has governed the presidential action. Such instances can be accounted for in a mixed or residual category that for convenience can be considered *mixed agenda* actions.

In terms of judicial appointments, both the *policy agenda* and the *partisan agenda* must be seen within the context of the tradition of primarily appointing members of the president's party. An administration whose judicial appointments are guided primarily by its *partisan agenda*, however, does not view the actions of the courts as central to its policy agenda and as a consequence judicial appointments are based more on partisan political considerations than considerations of ideology or judicial philosophy. The Truman administration is an excellent example of the primacy of the partisan agenda in judicial appointments that ranged from the Supreme Court appointments of conservatives Fred Vinson, Harold Burton, Sherman Minton, and Tom Clark, to an ideological hodgepodge of liberal and conservative lower court appointments including the first black American ever to serve on a federal appeals court (William Hastie), the first woman appointed to a lifetime federal district court position (Bernice Shelton Matthews), as well as appointments to supporters of racial segregation. What united these appointees was their affiliation with the Democratic party and the Truman administration's commitment to further its partisan agenda through judicial appointments.

An administration whose judicial appointments are guided primarily by its *policy agenda* will view the courts as important to the achievement of its policy goals *and therefore the necessity for a change in court policy* and as a consequence will use the selection process to appoint those who share its policy perspective. The Reagan administration is an excellent example of the use of judicial appointments to further the policy agenda.

It is reasonable at this point to inquire, assuming the validity of the policy and partisan agenda distinction, as to what conditions set apart administrations that use judicial appointments primarily to further their policy agenda from administrations that select judges primarily to further their partisan agenda. Let me suggest as a general proposition that when the party system is in flux, the constitutional policies of the federal courts will tend to be seen as out of step with the emerging new party system, resulting in policy agenda considerations rather than partisan agenda considerations dominating judicial appointments. For purposes of this analysis I will consider the period of the Jeffersonian party's ascendancy in the election of 1800, the Jacksonian triumphs in 1828 and 1832, the election of Lincoln in 1860, the elections of McKinley in 1896 and McKinley and Theodore Roosevelt in 1900, FDR's victory in 1932, and to some extent Nixon's election in 1968 and Reagan's in 1980 as signaling the breakup of the old party system and the ushering in of a new political era.[4] Court appointments during a period of party system stability, however, can be expected to be partisan agenda appointments even when a deviating presidential election has temporarily placed in power the party that is not the dominant party of the political era. We shall return to these propositions as we survey the historical evidence shortly.

It is necessary to distinguish between appointments to the Supreme Court and appointments to the major lower federal courts, that is, the federal district courts and the federal courts of appeals. Historically, the president has had the most latitude with Supreme Court appointments and the least with federal district court appointments because senators of the president's party have considered district judgeships to be political patronage for them to dispense. Appointments to the courts of appeals have fallen somewhere in between.[5] The best available evidence for testing these propositions concerns the Supreme Court,[6] whereas the evidence concerning the lower courts is incomplete and fragmentary.

THE HISTORICAL EVIDENCE

It is appropriate to start with the emerging party system that became apparent during the Washington and Adams presidencies. It is no accident that only Federalists were named to the Supreme Court. Acknowledging of course the rudimentary state of political parties in the 1790s, we can note that during Washington's administration and the first half of the Adams presidency there was what we might call a stable party system and it can be argued that Washington's ten Supreme Court appointments (those confirmed who served on the Court) were clearly of the partisan agenda kind. Considering that in the early years of the Court there was little for the justices to do (they decided no cases during the first three years of the Court's existence) this is perhaps not surprising.

Adams named three Federalists to the Supreme Court including John Marshall to the chief justiceship. Marshall's appointment occurred after the election of 1800 but before Jefferson took power. Partisan agenda considerations can also be seen to account for appointments to the lower federal courts, particularly those created by the Judiciary Act of 1801, the famous "midnight judges." Certainly Thomas Jefferson recognized this when he wrote to Madison, "The Federalists . . . have retired into the judiciary as a stronghold . . . and from that battery all the works of Republicanism are to be beaten down and erased."[7]

Jefferson's presidency began what historians consider the first party system that lasted until the Jacksonian period. Early in Jefferson's administration, John Marshall confronted President Jefferson in *Marbury* v. *Madison*.[8] Although Marshall is thought of as having emerged triumphant with the establishment of judicial review, the reality, of course, was that Jefferson won a political victory, Marshall's brilliant opinion notwithstanding, and the very next week the Court ate more crow by upholding the Jeffersonians' repeal of the Judiciary Act of 1801.[9] The Marshall Court took a backseat for the remainder of the first party system era.[10]

As Henry Abraham has noted in his extensive review of the historical evidence, Jefferson's three Supreme Court appointments were designed to counter the influence of John Marshall and as such were policy agenda appointments.[11] However, the total of four appointments made by Madison, Monroe, and John Quincy Adams were not. Despite the personal antagonisms between Thomas Jefferson and his distant cousin John Marshall, Supreme Court policy-making, thanks in large part to the skill and political acumen of Marshall, was not controversial and the Marshall Court did not strike down *any* act of Congress or portion thereof after striking down in *Marbury* v. *Madison* the trivial provision Marshall purported to see within section 13 of the Judiciary Act of 1789. Although once he left the presidency Jefferson professed dismay with the Marshall Court's national supremacy decisions, interestingly not much complaint was heard from the Jeffersonian occupants of the White House.

Kermit Hall, a historian of nineteenth century lower court judicial appointments, suggests that kinship ties through blood or marriage to leading Jeffersonian Republican congressmen played a large role in the selection of the several dozen lower court judgeships during the first party system.[12] This, too, is consistent with the partisan agenda appointment thesis for a relatively stable party system. It should also be observed that until 1853 lower court judicial appointments, considered judicial patronage, were administratively handled by the secretary of state. In 1853, the attorney general took over the responsibility for judicial patronage.

The Jacksonian era produced the second party system with the new Democratic party positioning itself as the champion of democracy for the lower classes and the enemy of privilege and wealth. In terms of its policy agenda, Jackson's administration was sympathetic to states' rights in the economic and social welfare regulatory spheres. A property-oriented and federal supremacy-minded Marshall Court was thus inconsistent with the spirit of Jacksonian democracy. While Marshall Court decisions did not directly clash with the Jackson administration and, in fact, in several key decisions appeared to be conciliatory to the Jackson position, Jackson nevertheless can be seen to have used his appointment power to further his policy agenda.

Of Jackson's five Supreme Court appointees, the appointment of Roger B. Taney as chief justice to replace John Marshall was the most prominent of the policy agenda appointments. After the Jackson appointees were in place, Justice Story lamented to his friend Senator Daniel Webster "the Supreme Court is *gone.*"[13] And so it seemed in a series of key decisions in 1837 in which the Taney Court was markedly less sympathetic to the arguments of business and more sympathetic to state regulation than John Marshall would have been, according to none other than Justice Story in his dissents.[14]

Hall, after studying Jackson's seventeen district judge appointments over Jackson's two terms, concluded that Jackson "appreciated that judicial decision making often reflected a judge's values. If possible, Old Hickory expected to know these before he submitted a nomination. He vowed to nominate a candidate only 'if his principles of the Constitution are sound, and well fixed.' "[15] Although Hall does not use the term, the weight of the evidence he offers in his detailed case studies suggests that Jackson's appointments to the lower courts (including not only district judge appointments but twenty-three territorial judges) were largely policy agenda appointments intended to affect court policy-making, although partisan considerations also played some role.

Once the new party system was in place, judicial appointments by Martin Van Buren became, in the words of Hall "more party directed than it had been during Jackson's administration."[16] Van Buren's seventeen lower court judicial nominations, unlike Jackson's, encountered (with only one exception), no opposition in the Senate. Although Van Buren was defeated for reelection in 1840, producing the first deviating election within a stable party system, Hall found that the twenty-two lower court nominees of Whig president Tyler were assuredly what we would call partisan agenda appointments geared to provide support for his reelection as a third party candidate. Tyler's successor, Democrat President Polk, "allowed the congressional wing of the Democratic party to mediate the selection process."[17] Polk's eight district court nominations as well as his two Supreme Court appointments were partisan agenda appointments.[18]

Whig president Zachary Taylor, the victor in a second deviating election, likewise, Hall found, "wielded . . . judicial patronage in an outwardly party-directed fashion."[19] His successor Millard Fillmore, taking over after Taylor's death in office, also used judicial appointments for primarily partisan purposes. His Democratic successor Franklin Pierce attempted to placate the northern and southern wings of the party and generally deferred to the congressional wing of the Democratic party. Buchanan's presidency occurred as the Jacksonian party system was breaking up. Although he wanted to appoint judges with a conservative view of popular sovereignty, judges that would be ideologically acceptable now that the Supreme Court had plunged into the slavery issue with its infamous *Dred Scott* decision[20] which Buchanan supported, Buchanan generally felt obliged to defer to Democratic senators loyal to him. He nevertheless was more policy-agenda oriented in his judicial appointments than his predecessors.[21]

The breakup of the Jacksonian party system in the 1850s, the election of Lincoln in 1860, and the onset of the Civil War brought about the third party system. Chief Justice Taney clashed with Lincoln, but Lincoln's three policy agenda appointments to the Supreme Court in 1862 helped assure a narrow five to four victory for Lincoln in the important *Prize Cases* of 1863.[22] Lincoln's appointment of Salmon P. Chase to the chief justiceship in 1864 can be attributed to a variety of factors, but undoubtedly it had a large policy agenda component. Suffice it to note that in the post-Civil War period the Republican-dominated Court refused to get involved in determining the validity of the Republican party–sponsored Reconstruction Acts.

After the Civil War, particularly with President Grant's election in 1868, the Republican party appeared to dominate a relatively stable party system. As for the Supreme Court, the Grant administration in 1870 appeared to make two policy agenda appointments to Justices William Strong and Joseph Bradley. These men were known supporters of the administration's legal tender policy which was being challenged before the Supreme Court. On the very day their nominations were sent to the Senate, the Supreme Court handed down by a vote of four to three an anti-administration legal tender decision.[23] The two new justices, however, joined the three dissenters to form a new majority the next year which overturned the 1870 decision.[24] Because the nominations were made before the Court had handed down its anti-administration legal tender decision, we cannot assert that President Grant was motivated by an intent to change a Court policy that had yet to be announced. As such, the Strong and Bradley appointments do not strictly meet our definition of policy agenda appointments, yet clearly policy as well as partisan considerations were involved in these appointments.[25] These appointments should therefore be considered mixed agenda appointments.

A reading of the Hayes, Garfield, Arthur, and Harrison appointees, particularly to the Supreme Court, suggests that partisan agenda considerations dominated their judicial appointments.[26] The same can be said for the appointments of Democrat Grover Cleveland in his two separate terms as president. The election of Democrat Cleveland in a Republican era, albeit an era of closely contested presidential elections, can be considered a deviating election. But Cleveland did not see the federal courts in general or the Supreme Court in particular as out of sync with his policy agenda, which in many respects was similar to that of his Republican predecessors.

Cleveland's four appointments to the Supreme Court, while all Democrats, were conservative in their economic views and were not intended to produce major policy shifts in the Court. They included the first former confederate official to sit on the Court, Lucius Q. C. Lamar of Mississippi; conservative Chicago lawyer and Democratic party activist Melville W. Fuller to the chief justiceship who presided over a vigorously economic laissez-faire Court, and is perhaps best known as the author of decisions emasculating the Sherman Anti-Trust Act[27] and ruling the federal income tax law unconstitutional;[28] Edward D. White, another conservative southern Democrat, a former confederate soldier and a Roman Catholic who would eventually be elevated to the chief justiceship by President Taft; and Rufus Peckham, who had been a close political ally of Cleveland's, was a former railroad and corporation lawyer, and who is best known today as the writer of the opinion of the Court in the infamous *Lochner* v. *New York*[29] decision, striking down New York State's maximum hours law for bakers and confectionary workers. None of Cleveland's thirty-four lower court appointments went to a Republican and there is no evidence to suggest that traditional political patronage considerations within the partisan agenda did not dominate the judicial appointment process.

When we turn to the 1896 election we see the Democratic party and the populists joining forces transforming the party battle and producing the fourth party system that lasted until the Great Depression. There are somewhat mixed results in terms of policy agenda versus partisan agenda appointments. The Republican party was victorious in 1896 and solidified its political hold on the transformed party system. The Supreme Court, however, was seen by the progressive wing of the Republican party as being hostile to efforts by government to regulate the excesses of capitalism, while the Republican party establishment was supportive of the Court's work. With the incorporation of the Progressive movement into the Republican Party, facilitated by Theodore Roosevelt's assumption of the presidency in September 1901 after the assassination of President William McKinley, policy agenda considerations became important at least for Supreme Court appointments.

When Theodore Roosevelt was faced with making his first appointment to the Supreme Court he most assuredly had policy agenda concerns on his mind as he indicated in a letter to Massachusetts senator Henry Cabot Lodge concerning the possibility of nominating to an associate justiceship Oliver Wendell Holmes, who was then serving as Chief Justice of the Massachusetts Supreme Judicial Court. Roosevelt wrote to Lodge that before naming Holmes "I should like to know that Judge Holmes was in entire sympathy with your views and mine . . . before I would feel justified in supporting him."[30] The evidence suggests that Roosevelt wanted to place progressives on the Court. Although Holmes had never been an activist in the Progressive movement or politically identified with it, his judicial philosophy was such that he became the leader of the Court's progressive or liberal wing.

Roosevelt's second Supreme Court appointment went to William Day, a progressive-minded jurist on the Sixth Circuit Court of Appeals, who had previously served as McKinley's secretary of state. Justice Day's performance on the Court undoubtedly pleased Roosevelt with his votes supporting government antitrust prosecutions and his dissent in the *Lochner* case.[31] Roosevelt's third Supreme Court appointee was William Moody, a Roosevelt Progressive and Roosevelt's attorney general. Moody's career on the Court, however, was cut short by illness. It is not known to what extent Moody as attorney general and Roosevelt as president screened lower court appointments in terms of the policy agenda. We do know that Roosevelt made sixty-nine lower court appointments, of whom two were Democrats and one was an independent.

The evidence for the Taft administration suggests that he took an active interest in the policy outlook as well as the legal ability of his appointees, but there is no indication that he saw the courts as a barrier to achieving his policies. Taft's judicial appointments were not meant to change court policy-making but rather keep it within acceptable parameters. He was not above naming Democrats and, in fact, three of his six Supreme Court appointees were Democrats. Daniel McHargue who studied Taft's Supreme Court appointments concluded that "All six of Taft's appointees in large measure shared his 'real politics,' though only half of them shared his 'nominal politics' in the sense of partisan affiliation. They would probably not have been considered for appointment had not their fundamental political and economic views been closely akin to those of the President." [32] Taft also named thirty-nine lower court judges, thirty-four of whom were Republican. Five Democrats were appointed to southern federal district court positions. [33]

Woodrow Wilson's electoral victories in 1912 and 1916, being deviating elections, might be expected to have resulted in partisan appointments. This appears to be so for the lower courts and it is relevant to observe that in his eight years in the White House, Wilson did not name even one Republican. To the Supreme Court, however, Wilson named his attorney general, Tennessean James McReynolds, who became one of the most virulently reactionary justices on the Court. This seemed to have been a partisan agenda appointment, satisfying to the southern base of the party and also resolving some difficulties within the cabinet due largely to McReynolds's curmudgeon personality. But Wilson also appointed two progressives, Louis Brandeis and John Clarke, and what we know of the politics of their appointments it would seem that policy agenda considerations dominated the Brandeis appointment and played a large part in the Clarke appointment. [34]

The return to normalcy of the 1920s, with Harding, Coolidge, and Hoover, saw the appointment of primarily Republicans. Harding's lower court record was exclusively Republican. Hoover, on the other hand, with the aid of Attorney General William Mitchell, attempted to break the grip that Republican senators had on district court appointments. But the purpose was to raise the quality of the appointees, not to change court policy. This led to several battles with Republican senators and ultimately to an administration retreat.[35]

Harding's appointees to the Supreme Court can be considered to have been primarily attuned to his partisan agenda, but this also meant a concern with policy in that justices sharing the dominant conservative wing's views were given appointments. Certainly Harding's appointment of Democrat Pierce Butler to the Supreme Court would have been impossible had Butler not been a sound economic conservative.[36] Hoover's appointments, occurring after the start of the Depression, can also be seen as attempts to pursue his partisan agenda. The appointment of Charles Evans Hughes to the chief justiceship was both a quality appointment and a nod to the Republican establishment, although it took a battle in the Senate to win confirmation. Hoover's next Supreme Court nominee was that of a southern Republican, fourth circuit judge, John J. Parker, whose nomination was rejected by the Senate because he was seen by his opponents as biased against organized labor and against black Americans.[37] Hoover was more successful with Owen J. Roberts, an establishment Republican lawyer from Philadelphia. Hoover's third appointment was one of the most remarkable in the history of judicial appointments.

Although the story is too long to recount here, Hoover in 1932 named a Jewish liberal Democrat, New York Court of Appeals Chief Judge Benjamin Cardozo, and Cardozo's nomination was unanimously confirmed by the Senate.[38] This was not a policy agenda appointment.

The election of Franklin D. Roosevelt in 1932 was a watershed election that set the fifth party system in motion. The New Deal program was based on premises of constitutional power allocated to Congress and to the president that were at odds with much of then current Supreme Court policy. The Supreme Court and the New Deal were on a collision course that culminated in the Court striking down eight out of ten major administration measures or actions within a sixteen-month period. The doctrines announced in those decisions threatened to destroy still other New Deal programs such as social security, unemployment compensation, the establishment of rights of organized labor enforced by the federal government, and, in general, the regulation of the national economy. Judicial policy-making became a major partisan issue.

The federal courts in general and the Supreme Court in particular were seen by the Roosevelt administration, particularly after 1934, as crucial to the success of the New Deal. Every one of Roosevelt's nine appointments to the Supreme Court, beginning with Hugo Black in 1937, was a supporter of the New Deal and shared a judicial philosophy of restraint in the realm of economic and social welfare policy-making with deference to the democratically elected branches of government. Surprisingly, although the Roosevelt administration has been the subject of extensive study by historians and political scientists, its lower court appointments have not been subjected to much systematic analysis. We do know that during Roosevelt's first two terms, he did not name even one Republican to judicial office.[39] Joseph Harris, in his classic study of the senatorial confirmation process, was of the opinion that Roosevelt's 125 federal district court appointments were partisan agenda appointments.[40] But given the nature of the party battle over economic and social welfare policy, particularly as it emerged during and after the congressional elections of 1934, it appears that the Roosevelt administration undertook at least some policy agenda screening of judicial nominees to the district courts.

The evidence for this can be found in the work of Richard K. Burke who studied judicial selection politics between 1921 and 1955.[41] Burke had access to the Justice Department files of many of the Roosevelt appointees and other appointees who no longer were serving on the bench by the mid-1950s when he did this research. Burke found that ideology played the greatest role in the appointments of Roosevelt. At the district court level, Burke found that Roosevelt used his power of appointment to reward New Deal supporters. But Roosevelt also made some appointments to conservative Democrats who were backed by political machines that supported Roosevelt.[42]

As for the appeals courts, the evidence suggests a more systematic approach to policy agenda screening by the Roosevelt administration. Burke's analysis of appeals court appointments concluded that ideology played a major role in Roosevelt's appointments, particularly between 1935 and 1940. Appeals court appointees had to be supporters of the New Deal and their judicial philosophy had to be compatible with that favored by the administration. Burke found that the administration took the initiative in numerous instances of recruiting appeals court judges. Roosevelt named fifty persons to the circuit courts, including three Republicans.[43]

My analysis of Justice Department files of all appeals court judges who served at any time during the 1961–1963 period shows that seventy-five percent of the Roosevelt appointees' files contained references to their policy or ideological views.[44] This was a higher proportion than that of actively serving judges appointed by other presidents. The Truman appointees had the lowest proportion of policy agenda references (17 percent), the proportion of Eisenhower appointees was 26 percent, and for the Kennedy appointees it was 43 percent. My study also indicated that not only were there references in the files to policy or ideology, but that the Roosevelt administration more than any other administration appeared to have the most concern with this.

The Truman administration, as suggested earlier, made partisan agenda appointments to all levels of the federal courts. Truman's judicial appointees accepted the by then well-established judicial precedents of the Roosevelt Court in the economic and social welfare domain and the federal courts were not a source of political controversy nor were they ordinarily seen by the administration as crucial to the success of Truman's domestic program. Truman named twenty-six to the courts of appeals, including the first black American, but as Burke concluded "there was little or no emphasis on administration service or ideology which so typified a number of Roosevelt's appointments."[45] Truman appointed ninety-one persons to the federal district bench, including the first woman.

The 1952 and 1956 elections of Eisenhower can be considered deviating elections and certainly insofar as judicial appointments were concerned followed the predominant historical pattern by resorting to partisan agenda appointments. It is said that after he left the White House, Eisenhower confessed to "my two biggest mistakes—and they are both on the Supreme Court,"[46] referring to the great liberal justices Chief Justice Earl Warren and Justice William Brennan. But when Eisenhower made these appointments, policy agenda considerations were not on his or his advisers' minds. The evidence also suggests that Eisenhower's three other Supreme Court appointments also were not policy agenda appointments.[47]

As for the courts of appeals, the Eisenhower administration named forty-five men, including forty-three Republicans and two Democrats. Harold Chase in his study of judicial appointments[48] interviewed William Rogers and Lawrence Walsh who each had served as deputy attorney general in the Eisenhower administration with responsibility for judicial selection and both told Chase that they did not check the political philosophy of a nominee nor did they think it ordinarily of importance.[49] Walsh said the same to me in an interview in 1964.[50] My review of the Justice

Department files of the Eisenhower administration found that in ten out of thirty-eight files of those in active service in 1964 there were references to the policy of ideological views of the appointees.[51] Of these, in at least three instances there was evidence of the Justice Department informally checking on the views of the appointees to make sure that they were not extremists (that is, extremists on the Left or extreme racists). In a general sense Walsh was probably referring to these instances when he told Chase: "I do not believe the political slant of a judge should be important unless it is so severe and dogmatic that it would cast doubt upon his temperament and intellectual capacity."[52] The Eisenhower administration named several liberal southern Republicans to the Fifth Circuit bench (Judges Wisdom, Tuttle, and Brown) but also a racist Mississippian (Judge Cameron). The southern liberals proved to be crucial in the school desegregation cases before the Fifth Circuit in the 1950s and 1960s. In the other regions of the country, there was a mixture of mostly conservatives but occasionally a few moderates or liberals.[53]

There were 125 lifetime federal district court positions filled by the Eisenhower administration, of which nine went to Democrats.[54] Again, these appointments can best be considered partisan agenda appointments. Those who participated in the appointment process seem to agree that policy agenda criteria were generally not considered. One Justice Department official in the Eisenhower administration, Simon Sobeloff, who had been solicitor general before being appointed to the Fourth Circuit, told me in an interview:

> There is no cataloguing of biases or prejudices taken by the Justice Department. Instead, what is of concern is whether the man is a qualified lawyer, knowledgeable, has community standing and judicial temperament. If a man has been a judge, the Justice Department will look at the man's judicial record as part of the screening process.[55]

Note that Sobeloff referred to men which was no slip of the tongue. Only men, and to be more precise, only white men were appointed by the Eisenhower administration to the courts of appeals and federal district courts.

Turning to the Kennedy and Johnson administrations, it is important to recognize that it was in the 1960s that the Warren Court made most of its great civil liberties advances, including the expansion of the rights of those accused of crime, the definition of what constitutes establishment of religion, finding a constitutional right to privacy within various provisions of the Bill of Rights, adjudicating the issue of malapportioned legislative districts and laying down the principle of one person, one vote, and furthering racial equality. While many of its decisions were highly controversial, notably in the criminal procedures sphere, the civil libertarian thrust of the Warren Court did not conflict with the policy agendas of Kennedy and Johnson. Kennedy's appointments of Byron White and Arthur Goldberg were not intended to bring about a change in Court policy and there was no perception of the Warren Court being at odds with the Kennedy administration. Robert Kennedy maintained that both he and President Kennedy believed that White and Goldberg agreed generally with their views.[56] The same can be said of Lyndon Johnson's historic appointment of the first black American to serve on the Supreme Court, Thurgood Marshall, and of the appointment of Abe Fortas.

Kennedy named 103 persons to the federal district courts, including ten Republicans and the second woman appointed to this lifetime position. He was responsible for twenty-one appeals court appointees, none of whom were Republican and all of whom were male. Kennedy appointed the first black American to a lifetime federal district court position (James Parsons), as well as three others (Wade McCree and Spottswood Robinson to federal district court positions and Thurgood Marshall to the Second Circuit). Although civil rights for black Americans became an important item of domestic policy for Kennedy, in several instances that was not translated into southern judicial appointments because of the intense pressure from southern Democratic senators and congressmen who controlled the major committees in Congress. According to Victor Navasky, who served in the Justice Department during the Kennedy administration, the administration caved in on some occasions and appointed to the southern bench known racists or those not known to be sensitive to or concerned about racial justice.[57] For the most part, the evidence suggests that most of Kennedy's appointments were partisan agenda rather than policy agenda appointments.

Lyndon Johnson's lower court judicial appointments present somewhat of a different picture according to Neil McFeeley.[58] Although Johnson was sensitive to party politics he also had substantive policy concerns as they related to civil rights and the Great Society programs. For example, McFeeley found in the Johnson papers a handwritten note by Johnson on a memo about a potential nominee asking:

How is he on Civil Rights? Ask Ramsey [reference to then Deputy
Attorney General Ramsey Clark] to thoroughly explore background—
prior association in cases, etc., and give me memo before I act. I want
this on every judge.[59]

On another recommendation from the Justice Department for the Fifth
Circuit, Johnson wrote, "Check to be sure he is all right on the Civil
Rights question. I'll approve him if he is."[60] This was important for
appointments to the southern circuits where a struggle between liberal
and conservative judges over desegregation was ongoing in the 1960s.

McFeeley asserts "President Johnson was very much concerned with
the policy views and personal inclinations of his judicial appointees."[61]
Johnson's judicial selection team "sought those who shared the Johnson-
Great Society views, or who at least were not antagonistic to the basic
thrust of the Johnson administration. Especially important was a progressive stand on civil rights and economic issues."[62] But Johnson was also
sensitive to the wishes of Democratic party senators and party considerations. On balance, McFeeley concludes that "a significant percentage" of
the Johnson appointees "could be termed 'Great Society liberals' on the
bench."[63]

Johnson appointed 122 persons to the federal district courts, including
seven Republicans, two women, and five blacks. To the appeals courts he
named forty, including two Republicans, one woman (the second ever to
be appointed to the appeals bench), and two blacks. By 1968, the last year
of Johnson's presidency, the federal courts in general and the Warren
Court in particular were under attack by conservatives for the Court's civil
libertarian decisions. The nation was trapped in an increasingly unpopular
war. The economy was experiencing difficulty providing both guns and
butter and as a result suffered severe economic consequences, including a
sharp rise in inflation. The mood of the country was tense, particularly
after the assassinations of Martin Luther King, Jr., and Robert Kennedy.
And the Democratic party was seriously divided in part over the Vietnam
War and in part over its own ideology. The partisan battle shaped by the
New Deal seemed to be at an end. And the chances for a Republican
victory in the presidential election of 1968 seemed increasingly promising.
Within this context Chief Justice Warren went to the White House on
June 13 and met with President Johnson. According to a memo reporting
on that meeting, Warren said "that because of age, he felt he should retire
from the Court and he said he wanted President Johnson to appoint his

successor, someone who felt as Justice Warren did."[64] Johnson tried to elevate Abe Fortas to the chief justiceship, but Senate Republicans sensing a Republican presidential victory successfully mounted a filibuster and blocked the appointment.

During the 1968 presidential campaign the Warren Court's civil libertarian policies, particularly concerning the rights of criminal defendants, became the objects of attack by Republican candidate Richard M. Nixon and third party candidate George C. Wallace. They received a combined total of 57 percent of the popular vote and Nixon became president. While on the campaign trail Nixon promised to appoint conservatives to the Supreme Court and the implication was that he would also seek conservatives for the lower federal courts.[65]

Certainly for the Supreme Court, Nixon's appointments were clearly policy agenda appointments. The administration declared war on crime as a major domestic policy objective and the Supreme Court was seen as an obstacle to administration policy. In the early months of the Nixon administration Warren Earl Burger was chosen to succeed Earl Warren as Chief Justice, with the intent that more than the names be turned around. In a bold and unprecedented action the Nixon administration orchestrated a successful campaign to force Abe Fortas from the Court,[66] thus creating another vacancy that after two failed attempts was filled by midwestern conservative Harry Blackmun. Nixon's two other appointments went to Lewis Powell and William Rehnquist. With the exception of Nixon's avowed desire to place a southern conservative on the Court, presumably as part of the Republican party's courting of the South, it would appear that only policy agenda considerations played a part in these appointments. When running for reelection in 1972 Nixon boasted that his appointments to the federal courts made the Constitution "more secure" and he promised to appoint more "strict constructionists."[67]

Nixon's landslide reelection in 1972 seemed to confirm that the country was in a new political era, even if it did not conform to the criteria associated in the past with a new party system (for example, Democrats still controlled both houses of Congress). But the Watergate scandal was to undo the Nixon presidency and it appears that during this period, a preoccupied White House and Justice Department were more concerned with partisan agenda appointments than with policy agenda appointments. Nixon needed all the political support he could get. The Nixon record of lower court appointments consisted of 179 district court appointments, including thirteen Democrats, one woman, and six blacks.

Nixon's forty-five courts of appeals appointees were white males and all but one were Republicans. The appointments to well-qualified blacks appeared to be partisanly motivated to make the Republican party attractive to black voters.

When Gerald Ford took over the presidency a major domestic policy goal was to restore integrity and credibility to the executive branch including the Justice Department. The appointment of Edward Levi, dean of the University of Chicago Law School, to the post of attorney general gave the Justice Department a new image of professionalism that was reflected in Ford's judicial appointments. Although attention was paid to Republican senators, the Ford administration named an unprecedented proportion not from the president's party to the district courts (over 21 percent). Of the fifty-two Ford district court appointees, eleven went to Democrats, one went to a woman, and three went to blacks. Of the twelve Ford appeals court appointments, one went to a Democrat but all were white males. Ford made one Supreme Court appointment and that went to a moderate Republican Seventh Circuit judge, John Paul Stevens. Given the circumstances of the appointment it cannot be said to have been motivated primarily by policy agenda considerations. Since going on the Supreme Court, however, Stevens has been the third most liberal justice.

Gerald Ford arguably might have been elected president in 1976 had he not pardoned Nixon two years earlier. However the pardon, along with the serious economic recession of 1974–1975 and continuing economic problems, brought Democrat Jimmy Carter to the White House, although only after a close election. Whether or not we see Carter's one term as a deviating election, we can nevertheless see a pattern of partisan rather than policy agenda appointments.

The Burger Court, with the exception of its rulings concerning the rights of women, in general was a conservative Court at the time the Carter administration took office, yet neither the Burger Court nor the lower federal courts were seen as offering obstacles to achieving Carter's domestic program. The Burger Court carried on the Warren Court's racial equality policies although with some division on the Court. And it was the Burger Court not the Warren Court that decided *Roe* v. *Wade*,[68] the woman's right to an abortion decision. The Carter administration looked at lower court appointments as furthering the partisan agenda, which for a Deep South Democrat in the White House meant aggressive recruitment of blacks, women, and Hispanics regardless of their philosophical or ideological orientation. This was unprecedented and represented an historic breakthrough for women and minorities that not incidentally was designed to generate political support among these groups and among liberals in general, important constituent groups within the Democrat party.

Carter appointed a record number of women to federal district courts (over 14 percent of his 202 appointments and in absolute numbers twenty-nine). Close to 14 percent or twenty-eight (the actual number) of district court appointments went to blacks, and close to 7 percent of 14 went to Hispanics. At the courts of appeals level, close to 20 percent (or eleven) of his fifty-six appointments went to women and about 16 percent (or nine) went to blacks. Two Hispanics and one Asian-American went on the appeals courts. Carter did not have an opportunity to name anyone to the Supreme Court but Griffin Bell, Carter's attorney general, claimed in a conversation with me after he left office that had Carter had the opportunity, the first appointment would have gone to cabinet member and former appeals court judge Shirley Hufstedler and the second appointment would have gone to black American Wade McCree, former appeals court judge and Carter's solicitor general.[69]

Close to 93 percent of Carter's district court appointments but only 82 percent of the appeals court appointments went to Democrats. Most but not all of the Democrats appointed by Carter were liberal or at least moderate. Some conservatives, however, were appointed, and they were for the most part sponsored by conservative Democratic senators. At the appeals court level affirmative action was more important than ideology when, for example, the administration appointed a conservative Republican woman, a conservative Republican Hispanic, and an independent moderate black woman, among others.

Reagan's election in 1980 and his landslide reelection in 1984 were seen by some as establishing the post-New Deal political era that Watergate had put in abeyance. In terms of national politics, the 1980 and 1984 elections showed new voting patterns among young voters and other population groups that appeared to augur Republican party domination of national politics much like the earlier elections of 1968 and 1972, although some political analysts argued that dealignment rather than realignment of the party system had in fact occurred.[70] Ronald Reagan was compared to Franklin Roosevelt in terms of personal popularity, in terms of stimulating contempt and antipathy from a vocal minority opposed to his philosophy, policies, and intellect, in terms of having a policy agenda sharply divergent with the immediate past, in terms of having to deal with serious economic crises (and it should be noted that both Roosevelt and Reagan resorted to Keynesian economics), and in both viewing the judiciary as frustrating key elements of their domestic policy agendas.

Of course, there were also important differences between Roosevelt and Reagan. Roosevelt's New Deal had the support of Congress and the large majority of the American people. Reagan's social agenda, with the exception of the law and order issue, did not attract overwhelming support in Congress and in the 1986 senatorial election campaign Reagan was unable to prevent the Senate from coming under Democratic control for the first time during his presidency. The New Deal issues of Roosevelt touched the everyday lives of the American people in tangible material ways while Reagan's social issues, although perhaps tangible to some people, are for many Americans more symbolic. Nevertheless, the Reagan administration from the start of the first term began to use policy agenda considerations for its judicial appointments for the express purpose of changing court policy.

Although party platforms usually need to be read skeptically, the Republican party platform of 1984 may be the exception insofar as it concerned judicial appointments. It said in part:

> Judicial power must be exercised with deference towards state and local officials. . . . It is not a judicial function to reorder the economic, political, and social priorities of our nation. . . . We commend the President for appointing federal judges committed to the rights of law-abiding citizens and traditional family values. . . . In his second term, President Reagan will continue to appoint Supreme Court and other federal judges who share our commitment to judicial restraint.[71]

The second-term Reagan administration's Justice Department was led by Attorney General Edwin Meese III who was far more aggressive and outspoken than his predecessor in office William French Smith. Meese opened a public debate about the role of judges in interpreting the Constitution and argued for a jurisprudence of original intent.[72] He cast doubt on over sixty years of Supreme Court precedents in which various provisions of the Bill of Rights had been made applicable to the states through the Fourteenth Amendment. He seemed to slight the importance of the Civil War amendments, including the Fourteenth, and the intent of *those* framers to change the nature of our federal system with respect to federal responsibility for the basic civil liberties of Americans, a point made by Justices Brennan and Stevens in their rebuttals to Meese.[73]

The key to any turnaround in constitutional law and American jurisprudence lies with the Supreme Court. Ronald Reagan made four appointments, his first being the historic one of Sandra Day O'Connor. His next appointment five years later was the elevation of Associate Justice William Rehnquist to the chief justiceship and then the appointment of Antonin Scalia to fill the seat vacated by Rehnquist. Then one year later, on June 27, 1987, another vacancy opened up when Lewis Powell announced his retirement. The following week, on July 1, Reagan nominated Robert Bork, a brilliant and outspoken former law professor and then sitting appeals court judge who took issue with many of the civil liberties rulings of the Court. Bork's nomination proved to be a lightning rod for civil liberties and civil rights groups who mounted a vigorous campaign against Senate confirmation and were considerably aided by liberal Democratic senators including those on the Senate Judiciary Committee. When the dust settled, fifty-eight senators voted against confirmation and the nomination went down in defeat. Reagan then announced his intention of nominating Douglas Ginsburg, but the proposed nomination was shelved after it was revealed that Ginsburg had smoked an illegal substance when he was a law professor. Reagan was eventually successful, however, in placing on the bench Anthony Kennedy who was unanimously confirmed by the Senate on February 3, 1988.

The O'Connor appointment can be considered both a partisan and policy agenda appointment. Campaigning for the presidency, Reagan promised to appoint a woman to the Supreme Court and although the administration vigorously opposed affirmative action it did not practice what it preached in filling the first vacancy with a well-qualified woman who was also a known conservative, thought to be sympathetic to the judicial restraint philosophy favored by the administration.

On the Burger Court, O'Connor was either the second- or third-most-conservative justice. The most conservative justice on the Burger Court was William Rehnquist whose elevation to the chief justiceship was clearly a policy agenda appointment as was the appointment of Antonin Scalia who had previously been appointed by Reagan to the United States Court of Appeals for the District of Columbia. There can be a plausible argument made that some partisan agenda considerations also played a part in the Scalia appointment by the fact that Scalia is the first person of Italian-American heritage appointed to the Court and also a Roman Catholic,

ethnic and religious groupings to which the Republican Party has sought
to appeal. In his first term on the Court, Scalia, as expected, was firmly
with the conservative wing of the Court although Rehnquist still remained the most conservative justice on the Court despite his new role as
chief justice.

Reagan's fourth appointee, Anthony Kennedy, was a judge on the
United States Court of Appeals for the Ninth Circuit since being appointed by Gerald Ford in 1975. Kennedy was known as a conservative
Republican but unlike Bork he had kept a low profile, his court opinions
were narrowly crafted, and his public speeches were not provocative. His
nomination, coming after the contentious battle over Bork, did not ignite
a wave of opposition. Kennedy himself was diplomatic and managed to
satisfy liberals and conservatives with his responses during his confirmation hearing before the Senate Judiciary Committee. Nevertheless, the
appointment of Kennedy, a conservative Republican and a practicing
Roman Catholic whose church vigorously condemns abortion, can be
seen as a policy agenda appointment. Although Kennedy was not expected to bring to the Court the aggressive and brilliant conservative
intellectual force that Bork would have brought, Kennedy was expected
to join the conservative wing of the Court.

The Reagan record of lower court appointments suggests that policy
agenda considerations dominated appeals court appointments. The controversy in the summer of 1986 over the appointment of Daniel A. Manion
to the Seventh Circuit, and previous controversies over the appointments
of Alex Kozinski to the Ninth Circuit and former senator James Buckley
to the District of Columbia Circuit, highlighted the seriousness with
which the administration was determined to appoint those who shared its
philosophical outlook.[74] Of seventy appointees (that is, those nominated
and confirmed by the Senate) to the appeals courts[75] through the seventh
year of the Reagan presidency, there were no Democrats and only one
was not a Republican (he was chairman of the Conservative party of the
State of New York). There was one black appointee, one Hispanic appointee, and four women appointed. The Reagan record of minority and
women appointments was better than that of any other Republican president but poor in comparison to the Carter record.

At the district court level the Reagan administration engaged in what
likely can be considered the most intensive and in some instances pro-
tracted negotiations with Republican senators over district court appointments in the history of judicial appointments. Some of this became public

in the Manion controversy when the administration, having put the president's prestige on the line, traded district judge appointments favored by Republican senators but opposed by the Justice Department on policy agenda grounds for votes for Manion. There were also other instances, however, when the administration deferred to Republican senators such as Alfonse D'Amato of New York who was generally successful in obtaining judgeships for political moderates. Even so, it is probably fair to say that policy agenda considerations dominated most district court appointments.

The Reagan record for the district courts at the end of seven years stood at 253 appointments, of which thirteen went to women, four to blacks, twelve to Hispanics, and twelve to Democrats.[76] Only the record of women and Hispanic appointments exceeded that of all other presidents with the exception of Carter.

CONCLUSIONS

In light of our review of the historical evidence of judicial appointments (see table 2.1 for a summary concerning Supreme Court appointments), what answers can we now offer to the questions about the Reagan administration with which we began our inquiry and about the propositions offered about judicial appointments and the presidential agenda?

First, the weight of the evidence suggests that judicial appointments have always been linked to *a* presidential agenda. In this respect the Reagan administration acted no differently than every other previous administration.

Second, insofar as it is possible to differentiate between the partisan agenda and the policy agenda, and acknowledging some gaps in the historical evidence, the Reagan administration appears to have been unprecedented in the systematic manner in which it pursued the policy agenda with its judicial appointments at all court levels. Although the administration of Franklin Roosevelt is a close second, on the basis of the available evidence it seems that what the Reagan administration did in its systematic attempt to shape the judiciary went beyond anything we have seen in American history.

Third, the evidence supports the linkage of policy agenda domination of judicial selection to historical eras when the party system is in flux or transition.

TABLE 2.1

Supreme Court Appointments and Presidential Agendas*

	Partisan[a]	Mixed	Policy[b]
Washington	10		
Adams	2	1[c]	
Jefferson			3
Madison	1		
Monroe	1		
Adams	1		
Jackson			5
Van Buren	3		
Tyler	1[d]		
Polk	2		
Fillmore	1[e]		
Pierce	1		
Buchanan	1		
Lincoln		1[f]	4
Grant	2	2[g]	
Hayes	2		
Garfield	1		
Arthur	2		
Cleveland	2[h]		

Notes: * This table includes only those confirmed by the United States Senate who served on the Court.
[a] The political party system is most often stable when partisan appointments are made.
[b] The political party system is usually in transition when policy appointments are made.
[c] This was the appointment of Chief Justice John Marshall which took place in a period when the political party system was in transition.
[d] The political party system was generally stable but a deviating presidential election resulted in the election of Whigs Harrison and Tyler (who succeeded to the presidency upon the death of Harrison).
[e] The political party system was generally stable but a deviating presidential election resulted in the election of Whigs Scott and Fillmore (who succeeded to the presidency upon the death of Scott).
[f] The political party system was in transition when Lincoln appointed Chief Justice Samuel Chase.
[g] The political party system was stable at the time of these two appointments.
[h] The political party system was generally stable but a deviating presidential election resulted in the election of Democrat Cleveland.

Fourth, with the possible exception of the Wilson administration, it would appear that presidents elected in deviating elections are as partisan agenda-oriented even with Supreme Court appointments as those elected in normal presidential elections during a stable party system.

It is, then, when a new party system is taking or has taken shape that we can expect the policy agenda to be of the highest priority in judicial

TABLE 2.1 (*Cont.*)
Supreme Court Appointments and Presidential Agendas *

	Partisan[a]	Mixed	Policy[b]
Harrison	4		
Cleveland	2[i]		
McKinley		1[j]	
Roosevelt			3
Taft	6		
Wilson[k]	1	1	1
Harding	3	1[l]	
Coolidge	1		
Hoover	3		
Roosevelt	4[m]		5
Truman	4		
Eisenhower[n]	5		
Kennedy	2		
Johnson	2		
Nixon			4
Ford		1[o]	
Reagan		1	3

[i]The political party system was generally stable but a deviating presidential election resulted in the election of Democrat Cleveland.
[j]The political party system was in transition at the time of this appointment.
[k]The political party system was generally stable but deviating presidential elections resulted in the election and reelection of Democrat Wilson.
[l]The political party system was generally stable at the time of this appointment which went to a conservative Democrat, Pierce Butler.
[m]These appointments were made during Roosevelt's third term when the party system was stable.
[n]The political party system was generally stable but deviating presidential elections resulted in the election and reelection of Republican Eisenhower.
[o]The political party system was in transition at the time of this appointment which went to John Paul Stevens.

appointments, particularly (but not confined) to the Supreme Court. The policy agenda of a new Republican-dominated party system at the presidential level is to use the appointment power to achieve the turnaround in civil liberties policy that constituted the social agenda that emerged during the Reagan administration. If this comes about, it will be more than slightly ironic that in 1991, during the bicentennial of the ratification of the Bill of Rights, a Republican-dominated Supreme Court and lower federal judiciary will be undoing the civil liberties and civil rights precedents that for civil libertarians have given life and meaning to the first ten amendments to the Constitution.

NOTES

1. See, for example, the discussion and citations of numerous scholarly works in Sheldon Goldman and Thomas P. Jahnige, *The Federal Courts as a Political System,* 3rd ed. (New York: Harper & Row, 1985), pp. 134–84.

2. *The Status of Federalism in America: A Report of the Working Group on Federalism of the Domestic Policy Council* (Washington, D.C.: Justice Department, Office of Legal Counsel, November 1986).

3. The presidential foreign policy agenda does not figure in this analysis as the judiciary has traditionally deferred to the president in his formulation and implementation of foreign policy. See, for example, Christopher H. Pyle and Richard M. Pious, *The President, Congress, and the Constitution* (New York: Free Press, 1984), chapters 4 and 5.

4. See Thomas P. Jahnige, "Critical Elections and Social Change: Towards a Dynamic Explanation of National Party Competition in the United States," *Polity,* 3 (1971), pp. 465–500; Walter Dean Burnham, *Critical Elections and the Mainsprings of American Politics* (New York: Norton, 1970); Walter Dean Burnham, *The Current Crisis in American Politics* (New York: Oxford University Press, 1982), pp. 251–320. Bruce A. Campbell and Richard J. Trilling (eds.), *Realignment in American Politics: Toward a Theory* (Austin: University of Texas Press, 1980); James L. Sundquist, *Dynamics of the Party System: Alignment and Realignment of Political Parties in the United States,* revised ed. (Washington, D.C.: The Brookings Institution, 1983).

5. Harold W. Chase, *Federal Judges: The Appointing Process* (Minneapolis: University of Minnesota Press, 1972), pp. 3–47. Also see Rayman L. Solomon, "The Politics of Appointment and the Federal Courts' Role in Regulating America: U.S. Courts of Appeals Judgeships from T.R. to F.D.R.," *American Bar Foundation Research Journal,* 1984, pp. 285–343.

6. See, for example, Henry J. Abraham, *Justices and Presidents: A Political History of Appointments to the Supreme Court,* 2nd ed. (New York: Oxford University Press, 1985) and Leon Friedman and Fred Israel (eds.), *The Justices of the United States Supreme Court 1789–1969* (New York: Bowker, 1969).

7. As quoted in Benjamin F. Wright, *The Growth of American Constitutional Law* (Chicago: University of Chicago Press, Phoenix Books edition, 1967), p. 31.

8. 1 Cranch 137 (1803).

9. *Stuart* v. *Laird,* 1 Cranch 299 (1803).

10. This is not meant to slight the great constitutional law landmarks from the Marshall Court or John Marshall's magnificent contribution to the establishment of the Supreme Court as a policy-making institution of government. But it should be kept in mind that constitutional law cases accounted for only 5 percent of the

Court's business. See Charles Warren, *The Supreme Court in United States History*, vol. 1 (Boston: Little, Brown, 1926), p. 813, footnote 2. Also see David M. O'Brien, *Storm Center: The Supreme Court in American Politics* (New York: Norton, 1986), p. 204. None of the great Marshall Court decisions was inconsistent with the agendas of the Jeffersonian presidents of the era.

11. Abraham, *Justices and Presidents*, pp. 84–87.

12. Kermit L. Hall, *The Politics of Justice* (Lincoln, Nebr.: University of Nebraska Press, 1979), chapter 1.

13. Daniel Webster letter to Mrs. Webster, January 10, 1836, as quoted in Gerald T. Dunne, *Justice Joseph Story and the Rise of the Supreme Court* (New York: Simon & Schuster, 1970), p. 351.

14. See *Mayor of New York* v. *Miln*, 11 Peters 102 at 153 (1837); *Charles River Bridge* v. *Warren Bridge*, 11 Peters 420 at 583 (1837); *Briscoe* v. *The Bank of Kentucky*, 11 Peters 257 at 328 (1837).

15. Hall, *The Politics of Justice*, p. 5.

16. Ibid., p. 29.

17. Ibid., p. 62.

18. See Abraham, *Justices and Presidents*, pp. 107–9 and Hall, *The Politics of Justice*, pp. 60–73.

19. Hall, *The Politics of Justice*, p. 90.

20. *Dred Scott* v. *Sandford*, 19 Howard 393 (1857).

21. Hall, *The Politics of Justice*, pp. 131–50.

22. 2 Black 635 (1863).

23. *Hepburn* v. *Griswold*, 8 Wallace 603 (1870).

24. *Second Legal Tender Cases*, 12 Wallace 457 (1871).

25. Abraham, *Justices and Presidents*, pp. 127–28.

26. Ibid., pp. 131–51.

27. *United States* v. *E. C. Knight Co.*, 156 U.S. 1 (1895).

28. *Pollock* v. *Farmers' Loan and Trust Co.*, 158 U.S. 601 (1895).

29. 198 U.S. 45 (1905).

30. As quoted in John Schmidhauser, *Judges and Justices: The Federal Appellate Judiciary* (Boston: Little, Brown, 1979), p. 90.

31. Years later, however, Justice Day would write the opinion of the Court in *Hammer* v. *Dagenhart*, 247 U.S. 251 (1918), which struck down an act of Congress that sought to abolish child labor for children under twelve and to regulate the labor of older children.

32. Daniel S. McHargue, "President Taft's Appointments to the Supreme Court," *Journal of Politics*, 12 (1950), p. 509.

33. Evan A. Evans, "Political Influences in the Selection of Federal Judges," *Wisconsin Law Review*, 1948, pp. 334–35.

34. Abraham, *Justices and Presidents*, pp. 178–83. For Wilson's appeals court appointments see Solomon, "Politics," pp. 314–23.

35. Joseph P. Harris, *The Advice and Consent of the Senate: A Study of the Confirmation of Appointments by the United States Senate* (Berkeley: University of California Press, 1953), pp. 317–20.

36. For a detailed analysis of Butler's appointment, see David J. Danelski, *A Supreme Court Justice is Appointed* (New York: Random House, 1964).

37. See Peter G. Fish, "*Red Jacket* Revisited: The Case That Unraveled John J. Parker's Supreme Court Appointment," *Law and History Review*, 5 (1987), pp. 51–104.

38. For a brief account see Abraham, *Justices and Presidents*, pp. 201–5.

39. Evans, "Political Influences", p. 335.

40. Harris, *Advice and Consent*, p. 320.

41. Richard K. Burke, "The Path to the Court: A Study of Federal Judicial Appointments (unpublished Ph.D. dissertation, Vanderbilt University, 1958).

42. Ibid., p. 292.

43. It is noteworthy that Roosevelt made a historic appointment in 1934 of the first woman to be appointed to a lifetime federal judgeship. The appointee was Florence Allen to the United States Court of Appeals for the Sixth Circuit. The second woman appointed to an appeals court was Johnson appointee Shirley Hufstedler in 1968 to the Ninth Circuit. The first woman appointed to a lifetime federal district court position was Truman appointee Burnita Shelton Matthews in 1949 to the federal district court for the District of Columbia. The first and still only woman appointed to the Supreme Court is Reagan appointee Sandra Day O'Connor in 1981.

44. See Sheldon Goldman, "Judicial Appointments to the United States Courts of Appeals," *Wisconsin Law Review*, 1967, pp. 186–214.

45. Burke, *Path*, p. 231.

46. Abraham, *Justices and Presidents*, p. 7.

47. Ibid., pp. 259–62, 266–71.

48. Harold W. Chase, *Federal Judges: The Appointing Process* (Minneapolis: University of Minnesota Press, 1972).

49. Ibid., pp. 102, 109–10.

50. Interview with Lawrence Walsh, May 27, 1964.

51. Goldman, "Judicial Appointment," p. 207.

52. Chase, *Federal Judges*, p. 110.

53. In the East, Eisenhower appointed moderate or liberals including Bailey Aldrich to the First Circuit, Sterry Waterman and J. Joseph Smith to the Second Circuit, and Simon Sobeloff to the Fourth Circuit. In the West, Eisenhower appointed moderates Frederick Hamley and Charles M. Merrill to the Ninth Circuit.

54. See Sheldon Goldman, "Characteristics of Eisenhower and Kennedy Appointees to the Lower Federal Courts," *Western Political Quarterly*, 18 (1965), pp. 755–62.

55. Interview with Judge Simon Sobeloff, July 1, 1964.

56. James E. Clayton, *The Making of Justice: The Supreme Court in Action* (New York: Dutton, 1964), p. 52.

57. Victor S. Navasky, *Kennedy Justice* (New York: Atheneum, 1971), pp. 243–76.

58. Neil D. McFeeley, *Appointment of Judges: The Johnson Presidency* (Austin: University of Texas Press, 1987).

59. Ibid., p. 87.

60. Ibid.

61. Ibid., p. 88.

62. Ibid., p. 136.

63. Ibid., p. 138.

64. Ibid., p. 113.

65. See, for example, *New York Times,* November 3, 1968, p. 11.

66. For a brief account, see Goldman and Jahnige, *Federal Courts,* pp. 8–9. For a different perspective and an extensive treatment of the events, see Robert Shogan, *A Question of Judgement: The Fortas Case and the Struggle for the Supreme Court* (Indianapolis: Bobbs-Merrill, 1972) and Bruce A. Murphy, *Fortas* (New York: Morrow, 1988).

67. *New York Times,* October 16, 1972, p. 1.

68. *Roe* v. *Wade,* 410 U.S. 113 (1973).

69. Conversation with Griffin Bell, June 1, 1981.

70. In general, see the discussion in Stanley Kelley, Jr., *Interpreting Elections* (Princeton: Princeton University Press, 1983), pp. 122–25, 166–224.

71. As reprinted in *Congressional Quarterly Weekly Report,* August 25, 1984, p. 2110.

72. Edwin Meese III, "The Attorney General's View of the Supreme Court: Toward a Jurisprudence of Original Intention," *Public Administration Review,* 45 (1985), pp. 701–4. This was initially delivered as an address before the American Bar Association on July 9, 1985.

73. William J. Brennan, "The Constitution of the United States: Contemporary Ratification," address before the text and teaching symposium, Georgetown University, October 12, 1985. John Paul Stevens, address before the Federal Bar Association, October 23, 1985, Chicago, Illinois.

74. See the discussion in Sheldon Goldman, "Reagan's Second Term Judicial Appointments: The Battle at Midway," *Judicature,* 70 (1987), pp. 336–37.

75. These figures do not include the United States Court of Appeals for the Federal Circuit which is a court of specialized jurisdiction. Only lifetime appointments to courts of general jurisdiction are included in the statistics cited in this chapter.

76. These figures are for lifetime appointments to courts of general jurisdiction.

II

LEADERSHIP AND THE PRESIDENCY

B
RYCE ONCE observed that democracy, probably more than any other form of government, needed leaders (1891). Perhaps it is because of this need, that the institution of the presidency has always loomed large in American politics from the inception of our Constitution. With the experience under George III fresh in their minds, the potential vices of leadership dominated the thinking of the framers of the Constitution; to all of them, fear of monarchy and centralized authority were considerations of the executive office. The conflicting needs for strong leadership and institutional protections against excessive power have structured the evolution of the American presidency.

The virtues and vices of executive leadership have attracted the attention of traditional and contemporary political scholars. The writings of Montesquieu ([1748] 1962) and Locke ([1690] 1967), are often cited as having influenced the framers' thinking about the presidency and other institutions of American national government. It is in their writings that we find the origins of the fundamental contradictions from which the presidency has evolved. To guard against the concentration of power, the framers relied upon Montesquieu's doctrine of separated powers, producing a decentralized government with many overlapping authorities. Locke, alternatively, provided guidance concerning executive leadership. He held that executive powers required "prerogative," or the power to act with discretion for the public good, without the prescription of law and sometimes even against it. It is from this environment of separated powers and executive discretion, that the institution of the presidency has evolved. As Theodore Lowi has noted, all institutions are built on contradictions and these contradictions will not go away because they are the result of mixing highly desirable goals that do not mix well (1985).

While the decentralization of political authority in American government has reduced the threat of excessive executive power, it has also meant that the ability to lead has not been guaranteed to occupants of the Oval Office. Instead, the office has presented both opportunities and challenges to presidents seeking to lead. This thesis was most forcefully argued by Richard Neustadt in his classic *Presidential Power* (1960). To Neustadt, the president possesses many institutional advantages but exercises them in a context of separate institutions sharing power. Presidents must use their personal skills, their standing with the public, and the resources of their office to persuade other institutional actors to accept presidential leadership.

[51]

Steven Brams, Paul J. Affuso and D. Marc Kilgour consider aspects of the formal foundations of presidential leadership. In chapter 3, "Presidential Power: A Game-Theoretic Analysis," they examine the formal powers of the presidency to get a bill approved and to veto legislation. They observe that attempts to override presidential vetoes by the House and Senate have been rare historically, and very few of the overrides attempted were successful. These authors argue that a strategic advantage underlies the legislative powers of the presidency. Based upon their analysis, they estimate that the total power of the presidency in comparison to the two houses of Congress, in approval and disapproval of legislation, may be as high as 67 percent. It is clear, based on the analysis presented by Brams, Affuso, and Kilgour, that the influence of the presidency in policy-making can be great.

Tremendous variation in presidential leadership over time, however, indicates that we must look beyond strategic advantages and formal authorities to gain a complete understanding of the contours of presidential leadership between administrations. Public expectations about the presidency, and the qualifications and skills of those occupying the office, have served as extremely important determinants of presidential leadership. In chapter 4, "Presidential Nomination Processes and a Clash of Values," John Aldrich examines ambiguities in the presidential selection process that have, at different times, worked to enhance or restrain presidential leadership. The fundamental contradiction in presidential selection, Aldrich argues, concerns the issues being addressed in the selection process. "Are we concerned . . . over *who* is nominated or *how* it is accomplished?" This conflict over process versus outcome, according to Aldrich, is a conflict between different sets of values about what constitutes "good" presidential performance. At various times, the nation has sought an effective manager for the highest office. As such, the president has been expected to conduct government activities efficiently and pursue consensual goals. At other times, the nation has sought a strong leader. In these times, presidents are expected to set the nation's policy agenda, often taking sides on controversial issues. Presidential selection processes have often been embroiled in controversy and continually reformed, Aldrich tells us, because these processes have been asked to reconcile two desirable, but conflicting, values; the desire to select the best manager and the preference for a policymaker.

REFERENCES

Bryce, James (1891). *The American Commonwealth*. Vol. 3, 2d edition. New York: Macmillan.

Locke, John ([1690] 1967). *Two Treatises of Government*. Peter Laslett (ed.), 2d edition. Cambridge: Cambridge University Press.

Lowi, Theodore (1985). *The Personal President*. Ithaca: Cornell University Press.

Montesqueiu, Baron de ([1748] 1962). *The Spirit of Laws*. Thomas Nugent (trans.). New York: Hafner.

Neustadt, Richard (1960). *Presidential Power*. New York: John Wiley.

THREE

Presidential Power:
A Game-Theoretic Analysis

Steven J. Brams, Paul J. Affuso, and D. Marc Kilgour

INTRODUCTION

The Founding Fathers had a good deal to say about the relative power of the House and Senate in the debate over the Constitution. Thus, while considering the two houses to be "co-equal" branches in *Federalist* No. 63 (*Federalist Papers,* p. 388), Madison averred in No. 58 that the House would have "no small advantage" over the Senate (p. 358). Similarly, in No. 66 Hamilton indicated that the House would be "generally a full match, if not an overmatch, for every other member of government" (p. 403); in particular, he predicted that the House's "mean influence . . . will be found to outweigh all the peculiar attributes of the Senate" (p. 404).

Brams (1988) used the Banzhaf (1965) index of voting power to assess the predictions of Hamilton and Madison.[1] The superiority of the House over the Senate is supported by the Banzhaf index, and, moreover, corroborated by data indicating that the House, when it initiates either ordinary legislation or a veto override, more often gains the assent of the

We thank Gary King for helpful editorial suggestions. D. Marc Kilgour gratefully acknowledges the financial support of the Natural Sciences and Engineering Research Council of Canada under Grant No. A8974.

Senate than when the Senate initiates these actions and tries to gain the assent of the House. But although the theoretical index and empirical data agree on the relative power of the two houses, the president's Banzhaf power of 3.8 percent seems way out of line with the actual legislative power that most presidents exercise.

True, the president's Banzhaf power is 11.6 times that of an individual senator, and 26.1 times that of an individual representative. But the president's structural coequality with the *entire* House and Senate in the passage of legislation, and his qualified veto—enabling him to prevent the passage of a bill unless overridden by at least two-thirds majorities of both houses—would seem to put him in a class by himself. Indeed, one would expect that the president would be more powerful than either house, perhaps even as powerful as two-thirds of both houses. Yet what theory would imply this consequence, and how it could be corroborated empirically, are by no means clear.

Another well-known index of voting power, due to Shapley and Shubik (1954), gives the president a somewhat more reasonable 16.0 percent of all power in the tricameral federal system comprising the House, Senate, and president (wherein the president is considered a one-member house).[2] On the other hand, the Shapley-Shubik index is based on a rather implausible model of coalition formation—in which all orders of joining a coalition are considered equally likely (Brams 1975; see also Dubey and Shapley 1979; Lucas 1983; and Straffin 1983)—which seems not at all descriptive of how alliances between the president and members of Congress form and agreements are reached, or how two-thirds majorities in Congress coalesce, on occasion, in order to override a presidential veto.

In this chapter we shall propose the application of a voting power index, due to Johnston (1978), that is related to the Banzhaf index but makes a crucial modification in that it substantially boosts the power of the president. Briefly, the Johnston index, unlike Banzhaf's, distinguishes between being critical in a winning coalition when one is uniquely so and when one shares this critical role with other actors, in which case one's power is proportionately reduced.

We do not propose the Johnston index, however, merely because it elevates the president to a preeminent position, seemingly more commensurate with his actual power in the federal system. Rather, we believe that the Johnston index captures, better than any other index, a feature of power that explains why most presidents have been so successful in shaping legislation and, even when opposed by majorities in both houses of Congress, preventing their vetoes from being overridden.

To begin our analysis, we shall propose criteria for measuring the *formal* power of an actor—that is, the power conferred on him or her by the rules for enacting bills or resolutions in either a single voting body or a set of interlocking institutions like the U.S. federal system (as specified in the Constitution). We shall not only show that the Johnston index satisfies these criteria but also argue, using a simple hypothetical example, that it gives more plausible numerical results than the Banzhaf index in certain situations.

Next we shall illustrate the application of the Johnston index to the federal system in two cases: (1) when a bill has a fifty-fifty chance of passage by each house of Congress; and (2) when a bill, vetoed by the president, has a fifty-fifty chance of being overridden in each house by two-thirds majorities. In these cases, each actor's probability of being critical is maximized, rendering comparisons among the different actors —the president, senators, and representatives—most meaningful. These are situations in which the outcome is most up for grabs; each actor will presumably exert himself or herself to the maximum in such situations, providing an acid test for comparing relative power.

The president's power, as we shall demonstrate, is different in these two cases. Consistent with the theoretical analysis, empirical data on the success of veto override attempts by Congress confirm the president's efficacy in preventing his veto from being overridden, though data that could be used to test the efficacy of the president in getting his legislation passed have not been analyzed. We conclude with some comments on the application of the Johnston index to the measurement of presidential power.

WHAT SHOULD A POWER INDEX MEASURE?

We assume, initially, that an actor is powerful to the extent that he or she

1. *alone* can decide outcomes; or
2. *alone* can prevent outcomes from being decided.

But there are few actors in the world who are dictators or hold veto power in the above senses, so it is appropriate to relax our criteria somewhat.

Thus, an actor might have a veto but not be the only actor with such a prerogative, as is true of the five permanent members of the UN Security Council. Their vetoes on the Council, as it turns out, give each 10.1 times as much power, according to the Banzhaf index (Brams 1975), as each of the ten nonpermanent members on the Council.

But this index probably understates the voting power of the permanent members. For whenever a permanent member can, by vetoing a resolution, prevent its passage, so can any of the four other permanent members. By comparison, whenever a nonpermanent member can, by changing his vote, prevent passage by the requisite majorty of nine votes (out of fifteen, which must include the five permanent members), so can three other nonpermanent members, not to mention the five permanent members. In other words, a permanent member shares his power with fewer other members than a nonpermanent member, which presumably reflects the permanent member's greater power.

We will not calculate here precisely the effects of this sharing, because it would take us too far afield from our study of a president's formal power. With this example in mind, however, let us add an additional criterion for measuring power: an actor is powerful to the extent that he or she,

> 3. *with the fewest other actors,* can decide outcomes.

In other words, the powerful may share their decision-making capability, but they share it with as few other actors as possible.

So far, we have not defined power. Roughly speaking, we mean by power having control over outcomes, with an actor's power increasing the fewer other actors exercise similar control.

More precisely, define a winning coalition to be *vulnerable* if, among its members, there is at least one whose defection would cause the coalition to lose. Call such a member *critical*. If only one player is critical, then this player is uniquely powerful in the coalition. Thus, a president in a coalition that includes himself, 52 senators, and 219 representatives (in each house, one more than a simple majority) is uniquely powerful.[3] If, however, a coalition comprises exactly 51 senators, 218 representatives, and the president, then the president—and everybody else in the coalition— shares power with $51 + 218 = 269$ other players. In this coalition, because a total of 270 players are critical, we assume that each has only $1/270$ of the power.

To define formal power, consider the *set, V,* of all vulnerable coalitions.

The *Banzhaf power* of player i is the number of vulnerable coalitions in which i is critical, divided by the total number of critical defections of all players, or i's *proportion of critical defections*. Mathematically expressed, for each vulnerable coalition $c \epsilon V$ (that is, c belongs to V), set

$V_i(C) = 1$ if i is critical c,
$V_i(C) = O$ if i is not critical in c.

The Banzhaf power of player i is defined to be

$$B(i) = \sum_{c \epsilon V} v_i(c) / \left[\sum_{j=1}^{n} \sum_{c \epsilon V} v_j(c) \right],$$

where $\sum_{c \epsilon V}$ represents the summation over all vulnerable coalitions in V, and n is the number of members (players). Thus, $B(i)$ is a fraction in which the numerator is the number of instances in which player i is critical, and the denominator is the total number of instances in which all players are critical.

To develop a second measure of power, first count the number of players who are critical in each vulnerable coalition c. Call the inverse of this number the *fractional critical defection* of that coalition, or $F(c)$. (Thus, if there are two critical members of c, $F(c) = \frac{1}{2}$.) The *Johnston power* of player i is the sum of the fractional critical defections of all vulnerable coalitions in which i is critical, divided by the total number of fractional critical defections of all players, or i's *proportion of fractional critical defections*. Mathematically expressed, for each vulnerable coalition $c \epsilon V$, set

$F_i(c) = F(c)$ if i is critical in c,
$F_i(c) = O$ if i is not critical in c.

The Johnston power of player i is defined to be

$$J(i) = \sum_{c \epsilon V} F_i(c) / \left[\sum_{j=1}^{n} \sum_{c \epsilon V} F_j(c) \right].$$

Thus, $J(i)$ is a fraction in which the numerator is the sum of i's fractional critical defections, and the denominator is the sum of all players' fractional critical defections.

It is worth noting that, for each vulnerable coalition, $c \epsilon V$, the summation of $F_j(c)$ across all players j, which necessarily includes all players who are critical in c, is one. By summing *this* summation across all $c \epsilon V$—in effect, reversing the order of summation given in the denominator of the above fraction—it can be seen that the denominator must equal the total number of vulnerable coalitions.

This means that the Johnston power of player i may be thought of as *the probability that, given a vulnerable coalition c is selected at random and then a critical member of c is chosen randomly, that i is that critical member*. This interpretation also extends to *sets* of members. In the federal system, for example, S might be the entire Senate; then the probability that *some* senator is the critical member selected by the above random procedure is

$$J(S) = \sum_{i \in S} J(i).$$

Before deriving the formal power of players in the federal system, we shall calculate the Johnston power of players in a simple weighted voting body to illustrate how it differs from the Banzhaf power. Consider the body [3; 2,1,1], which includes one 2-vote member and two 1-vote members, whom we call $2, 1_a$, and 1_b. The decision rule is a simple majority: 3 (out of 4) votes is the minimum number of votes necessary to make actions binding on all the members.

In this game, (2,1) is a vulnerable *arrangement*, or combination in which members of the same weight are indistinguishable. This arrangement subsumes two vulnerable *coalitions*, or subsets in which members of the same weight are distinguishable—one that includes one of the 1-vote members, $\{2, 1_a\}$, the other that includes the other 1-vote member $\{2, 1_b\}$ (see table 3.1). Similarly, (2,1,1) is a vulnerable arrangement, but it subsumes only one vulnerable coalition, $\{2, 1_a, 1_b\}$, which happens to be the grand coalition (that is, the coalition of all members).

The numbers of critical defections of the 2-vote member (3), and each of the two 1-vote members (1 each), in all vulnerable coalitions are shown in table 1, giving a total of five critical defections. Thus, $B(2) = \frac{3}{5}$ and $B(1) = \frac{1}{5}$. The fractional critical defections of the 2-vote member (2), and the two 1-vote members (½ each), sum to 3, so $J(2) = \frac{2}{3}$ and $J(1) = (\frac{1}{2})/3 = \frac{1}{6}$. Hence, the 2-vote member has *three* times as much formal power as either of the 1-vote members by the Banzhaf index, but *four* times as much by the Johnston index.

The reason, of course, that the 2-vote member does better according to the Johnston index is that it is uniquely powerful in the $\{2, 1_a, 1_b\}$ vulnerable coalition: it does not share its criticality with other members, so its power

TABLE 3.1

Banzhaf and Johnston Power in Weighted Voting Body [3; 2,1,1]

Vulnerable Arrangement	No. of Vulnerable Coalitions	Critical Defections (CDs)		Fractional CDs	
		2-Voter	1-Voter	2-Voter	1-Voter
(2,1)	2	2	1	$1/2 \times 2$	$1/2 \times 1$
(2,1,1)	1	1	0	1×1	0
Total	3	3	1	2	1/2
B(i)		3/5	1/5		
J(i)				2/3	1/6

is not divided. By comparison, in the (2,1) arrangement, where 2 appears twice as often as 1_a or 1_b, the two members of each vulnerable coalition share equally in being critical, giving each a fractional critical defection of ½.

We previously offered a probabilistic interpretation of power according to the Johnston index. The Banzhaf power of player i may be interpreted as *the probability that a randomly chosen critical defection is cast by i*. Thus, in the weighted voting body [3; 2,1,1], five critical defections are possible; given that these defections are equiprobable, the 2-vote member casts a randomly selected critical defection with probability ⅗.

Under the Johnston index, it is not critical defections that are equiprobable but vulnerable coalitions; once a vulnerable coalition is randomly selected, its critical members are taken to be equally likely to defect. In our example, the 2-vote member doubly benefits from these equiprobability assumptions: first, that a vulnerable coalition will be chosen (2 is in all of them); second, that a critical member within each will be chosen (2 is the only critical member in one of them).

But is it reasonable to assume that $\{2,1_a,1_b\}$ is as likely to form as either $\{2,1_a\}$ or $\{2,1_b\}$? Although vulnerable, $\{2,1_a,1_b\}$ is not minimal winning in the sense that *every* member's defection would cause it to be losing. To the degree that coalitions tend to be minimal winning, as Riker (1962) argues is the case in situations that approximate n-person, zero-sum games of complete and perfect information (the "size principle"), then the inclusion of $\{2,I_a,I_b\}$ in the definition of formal power would seem dubious.

Its inclusion seems especially problematic in the case of the Johnston index, because the 2-vote member derives from $\{2,I_a,I_b\}$ a full 50 percent of its fractional critical defections but only 33 percent of its critical defections. Yet this "problem" with the Johnston index, we contend, is precisely its virtue when applied to the federal system, in which information is often incomplete and imperfect, in violation of assumptions on which the size principle is based. For instance, a minimal winning coalition of exactly 51 senators, 218 representatives, and the president—in which 270 defections are critical—virtually never occurs.

Occasionally there is exactly a minimal majority in one house, making all its members critical along with the president, but on the vast majority of bills that the president signs, he is the only critical member. (When he vetoes a bill and his veto is overridden, he is never critical, which is a case we shall consider later.) The Johnston index accords the president unique power when coalitions in the House and Senate are not minimal winning, whereas the Banzhaf index assumes that such a critical defection counts no more than when the president shares his disruptive power with exactly 218 representatives, 51 senators, or all 269 legislators.

Because greater-than-minimal-winning coalitions are the norm in both houses of Congress, and because the president is uniquely powerful in these (except when these coalitions are two-thirds majorities in veto override attempts), we believe that the formal power of the president should—consistent with criteria 1 and 2 given earlier—reflect this unique role. When the president is not uniquely powerful, the president's power should, consistent with criterion 3, be reduced to the degree that this power is shared with other players.

There is another reason why players who are critical in coalitions that are not minimal winning can be thought to possess greater power. In a minimal winning coalition, every player is critical, making each player indistinguishable on the basis of criticality. As players are added to such a coalition (the added members are necessarily noncritical), some of the players in the original minimal winning coalition cease to be critical as well.

As long as some player is critical, the expanding coalition is vulnerable. In such an expanding coalition, the longer a player remains critical, the more essential that player is to its winning; conversely, the more easily replaced a player is, the less likely it is that this player will be critical (in large yet vulnerable coalitions, in particular). Thereby, the inclusion of vulnerable but not minimal winning coalitions in the definition of voting power is a way of measuring the "irreplaceability" of players, which we take to be a central feature of power.

In the next section, we shall show how the Johnston power of the president, a senator, and a representative can be calculated. For reasons that will become evident, we will separate this calculation into two cases, one involving the passage of bills signed by the president, the other the override of bills vetoed by the president.

The formal power of the president in these two cases will then be considered in light of veto data on conflicts between the president and Congress. To assess how often the president prevails when he vetoes bills, data on vetoes are suggestive though hardly conclusive. In the case of the passage of legislation, we indicate data that might be examined to test the validity of the Johnston index, but we have not attempted to collect or analyze such data here.

THE POWER OF APPROVAL AND DISAPPROVAL

The president, Senate, and House are interconnected by constitutional decision rules that allow for the enactment of bills supported by at least a simple majority of senators, a simple majority of representatives, and the president; or at least two-thirds majorities in both the Senate and House without the support of the president (that is, in order to override his veto).

To be sure, this conceptualization ignores the fact that a majority of the Supreme Court can, in effect, veto a law by declaring it unconstitutional (see note 2); and the countervailing power that Congress and the states have to amend the Constitution and thereby nullify Supreme Court rulings. Nevertheless, although other actors may affect the outcome, it seems useful to abstract those relationships among the actors having the most immediate impact on the enactment of bills into laws.

Consider now the number of combinations in which the defection of the president, a senator, or a representative is critical, and the fractional critical defections—or simply F's—that these combinations contribute to each player's Johnston power.[4]

1. *President.* One way for the president's defection from a vulnerable coalition to be critical is if it includes him, at least a simple majority of

senators, and at least a simple but less than a two-thirds majority of representatives (that is, between 218 and 289) — in order that the president can prevent the override of his veto in the House. This can occur in

$$\binom{1}{1}\left[\binom{100}{51}+\binom{100}{52}+\ldots+\binom{100}{100}\right]\left[\binom{435}{218}+\binom{435}{219}+\ldots+\binom{435}{289}\right]$$

ways. Let H be the number of supporters in the House and S be the number in the Senate. In each of the above arrangements, the F's of the President (p) are:

$F(p) = 1$, except when $S = 51$, $H > 218$, in which case $F(p) = \frac{1}{52}$;
   or when $H = 218$, $S > 51$, in which case $F(p) = \frac{1}{219}$;
   or when $S = 51$, $H = 218$, in which case $F(p) = \frac{1}{270}$.

A president's defection from a vulnerable coalition will also be critical when the coalition includes the president, at least a two-thirds majority of representatives (simple majorities were counted in the previous calculation), and at least a simple but less than a two-thirds majority of senators (that is, between 51 and 66) — in order that the president can prevent the override of his veto in the Senate. This can occur in

$$\binom{1}{1}\left[\binom{435}{290}+\binom{435}{291}+\ldots+\binom{435}{435}\right]\left[\binom{100}{51}+\binom{100}{52}+\ldots+\binom{100}{66}\right]$$

ways. The F's of the president are:

$F(p) = 1$, except when $S = 51$, $H > 289$, in which case $F(p) = \frac{1}{52}$.

2. *Senator.* For a senator's (s) defection to be critical, a vulnerable coalition must include exactly 50 of the *other* 99 senators (so that his defection would kill action by the Senate), the president, and at least a simple majority of the House, which can occur in the following number of ways:

$$\binom{99}{50}\binom{1}{1}\left[\binom{435}{218}+\binom{435}{219}+\ldots+\binom{435}{435}\right];$$

$F(s) = 1/52$, except when $H = 218$, in which case $F(s) = 1/270$;

or it must include exactly 66 of the *other* 99 senators (so that the focal senator's defection would kill action by the Senate in an override attempt), at least a two-thirds majority of the House, and exclude the president, which can occur in the following number of ways:

$$\binom{99}{66}\left[\binom{435}{290}+\binom{435}{291}+\ldots+\binom{435}{435}\right]\binom{1}{0};$$

$F(s) = 1/67$, except when $H = 290$, in which case $F(s) = 1/357$.

3. *Representative*. For a representative's *(r)* defection to be critical, a vulnerable coalition must include exactly 217 of the *other* 434 representatives (so that his defection would kill action by the House), the president, and at least a simple majority of the Senate, which can occur in the following number of ways:

$$\binom{434}{217}\binom{1}{1}\left[\binom{100}{51}+\binom{100}{52}+\ldots+\binom{100}{100}\right];$$

$F(r) = 1/219$, except when $S = 51$, in which case $F(r) = 1/270$;

or it must include exactly 289 of the *other* 434 representatives (so that the focal representative's defection would kill action by the House in an override attempt), at least a two-thirds majority of the Senate, and exclude the president, which can occur in the following number of ways:

$$\binom{434}{289}\left[\binom{100}{67}+\binom{100}{68}+\ldots+\binom{100}{100}\right]\binom{1}{0};$$

$F(r) = 1/290$, except when $S = 67$, in which case $F(r) = 1/357$.

In counting combinations in which a senator or representative is critical in an override attempt, we have implicitly assumed that the way he or she voted initially (that is, on the nonoverride vote) does not change. Indeed, for the purposes of this calculation, there is only one vote: a Senate or House member's power accrues from being critical in his or her house either when the president assents or when the president dissents (that is, casts a veto)—but not both. For if a senator or representative could be critical in achieving both a simple majority on the first vote and a two-thirds majority on the override attempt, this would imply that at least $\frac{2}{3}-\frac{1}{2}=\frac{1}{6}$ of the members of his or her house changed their votes on the override vote.

Counting both votes toward a senator's or representative's power would imply that a president can simultaneously sign a bill (making a member of a simple majority in one house critical) and veto the bill (making a member of a two-thirds majority in one house critical), which is obviously nonsensical. In counting critical defections, therefore, we assume in effect that all players vote the same way on both the original bill and the override attempt (if it occurs); this is equivalent to assuming that only one vote is taken.

In fact, however, the combinatorial contribution that the Senate and House veto override power makes to the Johnston (and Banzhaf) power of individual senators and representatives is negligible compared to the power that these players obtain from their nonoverride power. This is because, in order for the override to contribute to a senator's or representative's power, one house must have at least a two-thirds majority while the other House has exactly a two-thirds majority. In relative terms, this can occur in very few ways compared to getting less lopsided majorities.

The veto override ability of both houses, therefore, contributes only a miniscule amount to the formal power (Johnston or Banzhaf) of their members; their powers would be virtually the same if the House and Senate could not override presidential vetos by two-thirds majorities. Yet the veto power of the two houses *seems* significant—and, indeed, it can be shown to be so *if* separated from the members' ability to be critical in the passage of legislation (more on this later).

Based on the above calculations, the Johnston power values of the president, a senator, and a representative are:

$$J(p) = 0.770 \quad J(s) = 0.00156 \quad J(r) = 0.000169$$

For the entire Senate *(S)* and the entire House *(H)*,

$$J(S) = 0.156 \quad J(H) = 0.0736.$$

Thus, a senator is 9.22 times as powerful as a representative, which translates into the Senate as an institution being 2.12 times as powerful as the House. But it is the President, with 77 percent of the power, who is the truly dominant figure in the federal system, according to the Johnston index.

Before trying to assess the significance of these figures, we shall propose a separate calculation that better captures the power of players in situations wherein Congress attempts to override a presidential veto. We make this calculation for two reasons: (1) Congress's ability to override a presidential veto has essentially no effect on the Johnston (or Banzhaf) power of players, as just computed; and (2) the situation in which a presidential veto might be overridden is qualitatively different from one in which no override attempt is made.

To be specific, the Banzhaf and Johnston indices presume a situation wherein each player is equally likely to support or oppose the issue in question. This feature, coupled with the large sizes of the Senate and House, causes both indices to depreciate to insignificance instances of veto override because they are so unlikely to occur under the equiprobability hypothesis. In fact, if the Constitution were amended to end veto overrides, the president's power, as measured by either index, would increase by less than one ten-billionth (10^{-10}).

Clearly, an override attempt is not only likely to be made, but also will most hang in balance, when the probability that a senator or representative will vote to override the veto is $\frac{2}{3}$. In this situation of maximum uncertainty, each player will presumably strive to the utmost to affect the outcome, making this the acid test of power in veto override attempts.

We can modify our calculations to focus on the veto override process. This is most easily done by simply assuming that each senator and each representative has probability $\frac{2}{3}$ of supporting the legislation, and, of course, probability $\frac{1}{3}$ of opposing it. Our previous calculations are then modified term by term, with each count of Senate or House support multiplied by appropriate probabilities. Thus, for example,

$$\binom{100}{51} \text{ becomes } \binom{100}{51}\left(\frac{2}{3}\right)^{51}\left(\frac{1}{3}\right)^{49};$$

$$\binom{99}{66} \text{ becomes } \binom{99}{66}\left(\frac{2}{3}\right)^{66}\left(\frac{1}{3}\right)^{33};$$

$$\binom{435}{218} \text{ becomes } \binom{435}{218}\left(\frac{2}{3}\right)^{218}\left(\frac{1}{3}\right)^{217}.$$

In effect, we weight the combinatorial terms by the probabilities of getting the requisite numbers—on each side of the override vote—so as to make the president, a senator, or a representative critical. All other aspects of the calculations, including the counting of fractional critical defections, are unchanged.

The difference between the earlier "approval" (passage) and present "disapproval" (override) calculations is really one of degree, not kind. To see this, substitute the probability of $\frac{1}{2}$ for both $\frac{2}{3}$ and $\frac{1}{3}$ in the disapproval calculations. Thereby every combinatorial term is multiplied by $\frac{1}{2}$ raised to the same power (535), which can be factored out of the approval calculations. This means that the Johnston (and Banzhaf) indices, which measure the *relative* (passage) power of the different players, simply incorporate the implicit assumption of equal probabilities, which we could ignore earlier because they cancel out.

Both the passage and override calculations can be thought of as founded on *probabilities* that each player is critical. The Banzhaf index normalizes these probabilities so that they sum to one, giving equal weight to every critical defection. The Johnston index is based on a different normalization, giving greater weight to the defections of players who are critical with fewer other players. In addition, in the override calculation just described, wherein the most likely outcome is assumed to be a $2/3 - 1/3$ split in favor of override in each house, the combinations themselves are, in effect, weighted by this assumed split, whereas in the passage case they are (equally weighted) by an assumed $1/2 - 1/2$ split.

Does the president do better if the test of strength is on passage—when the probability that a member of either house will support him is $1/2$—or on override attempts—when the probability that a member of either house will support him is $1/3$? In either case, there are even odds in each house that the vote will go for or against the president, but the latter situation is definitely more favorable to the president, as the following Johnston power values for the override calculations show:

$$J(p) = 0.886 \quad J(s) = 0.000762 \quad J(r) = 0.0000856$$
$$J(S) = 0.0762 \quad J(H) = 0.0373$$

Compared with the passage values, the president jumps from 77 percent to 89 percent, and the power of the Senate and House as institutions are cut significantly (the Senate from 15.6 to 7.6 percent, the House from 7.3 to 3.7 percent). Intuitively, in the veto override case, the power of senators and representatives is shared on average with $2/3$ of their colleagues, depressing their power relative to the president's and that of the Senate and House as well.

In the concluding section, we shall consider the implications of these results, introducing some data on vetoes cast by presidents and sometimes overridden by Congresses. No systematic data on the passage of bills have been collected that might be used to compare with the theoretical calculations, however, so at this stage our results are quite tentative.

CONCLUSIONS

Our justification of the Johnston index rested primarily on the fact that it gives proportionately more power to actors the fewer other actors they share their criticality with in vulnerable coalitions. Secondarily, the Banzhaf index, which counts all critical defections the same, gives the president less than 4 percent of all power in the federal system, which seems inordinately low.

The Johnston index gives the president 77 percent of all power in the passage calculations, but it is hard to think of how this figure might be validated by data. Because it is based on the assumption that a vulnerable coalition forms, one might examine all roll calls in which there is a minimal majority in at least one house versus larger majorities in the two houses (in which case only the president is critical if the majorities are not two-thirds or greater).

In the latter case, the president is all-powerful, given that the majorities are not two-thirds majorities or greater against the president. In the former cases, the president must share his power, so the relative frequencies of these two cases—presumably on important bills—might give some empirical estimate of the likelihood that each player is critical, which could then be compared with the Johnston values.

Minimal majorities might be too strict a standard on which to base the power of senators and representatives. Close votes that are not minimal on bills the president supports might indicate situations, before the vote is taken, in which the president may well not prevail. In these situations, given uncertainty about the final tally, the president's power might also be considered less than total. His record is getting such legislation enacted, especially that which he takes a strong public stand on, might be taken as a measure of his passage power.

A final reckoning of the president's power versus that of the Senate or House (and their members) seems elusive, however, because it is not measured simply by roll calls and the closeness of votes. A host of other factors comprise what is usually meant by presidential power (Neustadt 1980). Nonetheless, close roll call votes, in which members of Congress may be critical, give us the opportunity to assess presidential power quantitatively and compare it with the kinds of formal calculations presented here.

The veto override calculation seems somewhat easier to relate to empirical data. Excluding "pocket vetoes" (41.3 percent of all presidential vetoes that have been cast)—whereby a president, by taking no action, prevents passage of a bill if Congress adjourns within ten days after the bill is sent to him—which cannot be overridden, the forty presidents from George Washington (1789–1797) to Ronald Reagan (through 1986) have cast a total of 1,406 vetoes. Only 98, or 7.0 percent, have been overridden by Congress in this almost 200-year span of time, suggesting that Congress's constitutional authority has not increased very significantly its effective power—at least to override presidential vetoes (Roberts 1986). This 93 percent success rating of the president, moreover, does not include cases in which the president's threat of a veto deterred Congress from even bringing up a bill for a vote.

When the president did veto legislation, one or both houses of Congress made the attempt to override only 256, or 18.3 percent, of the 1,398 nonpocket vetoes cast by presidents through 1984 (U.S. Senate 1978; U.S. Senate 1985). Of these, Congress was successful in overriding 40.6 percent. Although this is not a fantastic success rating in enacting legislation that the president opposed, it would appear that the bills on which an attempt was made to override a presidential veto were among the most important passed by Congress (Jackson 1967).

Overall, however, it seems fair to say that Congress's constitutional authority to override presidential vetoes has not dramatically augmented its control over legislation. In fact, almost half of all presidents (nineteen) never had a veto overturned, including John F. Kennedy (1961–1963) and Lyndon B. Johnson (1963–1969).

In short, presidents cast a large shadow, which suggests that their 89 percent Johnston power on override attempts may not be far off the mark. At a minimum, a president is probably the equal of the two-thirds majorities of Congress necessary to overturn his veto, giving him at least 67 percent of the power in the federal system. Perhaps with this reserve of strength in mind, Hamilton, in *Federalist* No. 73 (*Federalist Papers*, p. 445), strongly argued that the "qualified negative" (veto) was certainly preferable to an "absolute negative," in which the president would have all the (negative) power. Even with this limitation, Woodrow Wilson (1885, p. 52) characterized the president's veto power as "beyond all comparison, his most formidable prerogative," and this indeed appears to be the case.

Our formal calculations indicate that a president's power of both approval and disapproval exceeds 67 percent if power can be rooted in a player's criticality—diminished by others who also are critical—in vulnerable coalitions. Although we believe this notion of power is eminently reasonable, it still needs to be confronted by more and better data.

Previous empirical data, which are consistent with the Banzhaf index (Brams 1988) but not the Johnston index, show the House to be more powerful than the Senate. Generally, the smaller an institution (including the presidency), the more likely its members are critical with fewer others, which explains this descrepancy between Banzhaf and Johnston. But even if the Johnston index does not account for the relatively greater success of the House in conflicts with the Senate, it does show the president to be preeminent, which—while perhaps not exactly the intent of the Founding Fathers—seems by and large true today.

NOTES

1. The model of voting power employed by Banzhaf identifies "critical" members of winning coalitions. A member is considered critical or essential when its sole defection from a coalition would change that coalition from a winning one to a losing one. In Banzhaf's model, the power of one member relative to another member is proportional to the number of coalitions in which each is critical. Applying this model to the federal system comprising Congress and the president —whose relevant features will be described in detail later—produces the following Banzhaf power values:

President	0.03803
Senator	0.00329
Representative	0.00146

Insofar as the power of the Senate may be thought of as the sum of the powers of its 100 members, and that of the House as the sum of the powers of its 435 members, the power of the Senate and House, respectively, are 0.32881 and 0.63316, giving the House nearly twice as much power as the Senate.

2. Although a majority of the Supreme Court is able to declare legislation unconstitutional, thereby exercising a veto of a sort, we shall not consider the Court as an actor in the present analysis. Chamberlin (1988) has extended the Banzhaf calculations in Brams (1988) to the Court—showing it to be intermediate in power between the president and the House and Senate—but the qualitatively different role it plays in the federal system makes power comparisons with the other players somewhat questionable.

3. In fact, because the vice-president is able to break a 50–50 tie, 50 senators,

not 51, may constitute a simple majority—but only if the president, through the vice-president, favors this coalition of 50. The other 50-coalition is not sufficient to win—in fact, the tie-breaking vote of the vice-president will cause it to lose— so a simple majority for it will be 51 senators.

To avoid such considerations in measuring power, wherein the position of a president on a bill matters, we exclude the vice-president as a player from the subsequent analysis. This exclusion has virtually no effect on our later conclusions, though it should be borne in mind that the vice-president has the same defection possibilities as a senator when there is a 50–50 tie.

On the other hand, when the vote is 51–49, the vice-president is not critical, but a senator may be. Specifically, a senator's defection from the 51-coalition will be critical if the vice-president is on the side of the original 49-coalition (which becomes a 50-coalition with the defection), but not critical if the vice-president is on the other side.

In sum, the vice-president is always critical in a 50–50 tie but never critical when the vote is 51–49. By comparison, a senator may or may not be critical in either situation (depending on which side he or she is on), which probably makes the vice-president roughly equivalent to a senator in terms of voting power. But because the vice-president is really only a surrogate for the president in the role of president of the Senate, it is the president's power that is enhanced, albeit only slightly, over the figures to be given later.

4. In counting vulnerable coalitions, we use the standard notation for the number of combinations that can be formed from m objects taken n at a time, of $m!/[n!(m-n)!]$. The exclamation point (!) indicates a factorial and means that the number it follows is to be multiplied by every positive integer smaller than itself (for example, $4! = 4 \times 3 \times 2 \times 1 = 24$).

To illustrate the meaning of combinations with a simple example, suppose one wishes to calculate the number of ways of choosing a subset of three voters from a set of four, designated by {a,b,c,d}. Clearly, a subset containing three voters can be formed by excluding any one of the original four, yielding four different subsets of three voters: {a,b,c}, {a,b,d}, {a,c,d}, and {b,c,d}. In simple cases like this one, the number of subsets of a given size can thus be found by complete enumeration; in more complicated cases (like those to be developed in the paper), a direct calculation is the only feasible one. In our illustrative example, the direct calculation confirms that the number of combinations of four objects taken three at a time is

$$\binom{4}{3} = \frac{4!}{3!1!} = \frac{(4 \times 3 \times 2 \times 1)}{(3 \times 2 \times 1)(1)} = 4.$$

REFERENCES

Banzhaf, John F., III (1965). "Weighted Voting Doesn't Work: A Mathematical Analysis." *Rutgers Law Review* 19 (Winter): 317–43.

Brams, Steven J. (1975). *Game Theory and Politics*. New York: Free Press.

Brams, Steven J. (1988). "Are the Two Houses of Congress Really Co-Equal?" In *The Federalist Papers and the New Institutionalism*, ed. Bernard Grofman and Donald Wittman. New York: Agathon.

Chamberlin, John R. (1988). "Assessing the Power of the Supreme Court." In *The Federalist Papers in Public Choice Perspective: The New Institutionalism and the Old*, ed. Bernard Grofman and Donald Wittman. New York: Agathon.

Dubey, Pradeep, and Lloyd S. Shapley (1979). "Mathematical Properties of the Banzhaf Power Index." *Mathematics of Operations Research* 4: 99–131.

The Federalist Papers. See Hamilton, Alexander, James Madison, and John Jay.

Hamilton, Alexander, James Madison, and John Jay ([1787–88] 1961). *The Federalist Papers,* edited by Clinton Rossiter. New York: New American Library.

Jackson, Carlton (1967). *Presidential Vetoes: 1792–1945.* Athens, Ga.: University of Georgia Press.

Johnston, R. J. (1978). "On the Measurement of Power: Some Reactions to Laver." *Environment and Planning A* 10: 907–14.

Lucas, William F. (1983). "Measuring Power in Weighted Voting Systems." In *Modules in Applied Mathematics: Political and Related Models,* vol. 2, ed. Steven J. Brams, William F. Lucas, and Philip D. Straffin, Jr. New York: Springer, 1982, pp. 183–238.

Neustadt, Richard E. (1980). *Presidential Power: The Politics of Leadership from FDR to Carter.* New York: Wiley.

Riker, William H. (1962). *The Theory of Political Coalitions.* New Haven: Yale University Press.

Roberts, Steven V. (1986). "Key to Strategy: The Pocket Veto." *New York Times,* September 18, 1986, p. B10.

Shapley, L. S., and Martin Shubik (1954). "A Method of Evaluating the Distribution of Power in a Committee System." *American Political Science Review* 48 (September): 787–92.

Straffin, Philip D., Jr. (1983). "Power Indices in Politics." In *Modules in Applied Mathematics: Political and Related Models,* vol. 2, ed. Steven J. Brams, William F. Lucas, and Philip D. Straffin, Jr. New York: Springer, pp. 256–321.

U.S. Senate (1978). *Presidential Vetoes, 1789–1976.* Washington, D.C.: U.S. Government Printing Office.

U.S. Senate (1985). *Presidential Vetoes, 1977–1984.* Washington, D.C.: U.S. Government Printing Office.

Wilson, Woodrow (1885). *Congressional Government: A Study in American Politics.* Boston: Houghton Mifflin.

FOUR

Presidential Nomination Processes and a Clash of Values

John H. Aldrich

Alexander Hamilton argued that one of the chief virtues of the electoral college was that it afforded "as little opportunity as possible to tumult and disorder. This evil was not least to be dreaded in the election of a magistrate who was to have so important an agency in the administration of the government as the President of the United States" (1961, p. 412). The electoral college is but one of the many methods of nominating and, in this case also, electing the president that have been used in America. Since passage of the Twelfth Amendment to the Constitution, there has been relatively little change in the method of presidential election. The method of party nomination for president, however, has changed substantially and often, and controversy over such processes has been even more regular. That today's process (largely similar to that used first in 1972) is unique, complex, and apparently open to "tumult and disorder" indicates how far we have come since the Founding. And yet, for all of the various nomination methods that have been employed, today's process is no less (and probably no more) controversial than, say, "King Caucus" was in 1824.

The puzzle I wish to explore in this paper is why presidential nomina-

tion processes have been so various and, especially, so controversial. No
other electoral process in America has changed so often, nor is the fundamental basis of their methods so regularly attacked. Congressional nominations, for instance, were controversial at the turn of the century, but
with the adoption of congressional primaries (or, even in those states that
still use caucus-convention systems, with their continued use) controversy
over the method of congressional nomination essentially ended. Why,
then, have American political parties not been able to devise a method of
presidential nomination that could end controversy, that could, that is, be
accepted as legitimate and smoothly functioning?

The answer to this puzzle, I submit, resides in a clash of values over
the very nature of the presidency, and these values, which divide roughly
into two clusters, are, at once, both desirable and yet logically incompatible. Logical incompatibility does not mean that these values always conflict. It means that there is always the potential for their conflict, and the
controversial and changeable nature of presidential nomination processes
indicates how often these values do conflict.

The two views of the presidency are of the president as chief executive,
as manager and administrator of national government, and of the president as political leader, as agenda setter and most important source of
policy initiation in American politics. Surrounding both views of the
nature of the presidency are a cluster of (often loosely) related values that
manifest themselves in a number of ways. One important such manifestation is the process of nomination. Before turning to these views in a bit
more detail, two questions should be addressed. First, why is it the
presidential nomination process in particular that is the major source of
institutional controversy? Secondly, how are the competing views revealed in clashing values over that process?

As to the first question, the nomination process is not, of course,
constitutionally established. Since parties were not anticipated, the Founders did not imagine they had to consider such a question. As inventions
of practical convenience, the political parties are, in all ways, in constant
reinvention to address new political realities. Thus, so are their nomination procedures. Moreover, not only is the selection of the presidential
nominee the most important single act of the parties, but also it is the
nomination process that is the most important part of presidential selection in the sense that it serves most to reduce the field of aspirants, from
the full set of all those who desire office, to the two from whom one will
finally be chosen.

Concerning the second question, the essential conflict over values can be summarized by asking whether one is more concerned about selecting the best person to stand for President in some satisfactory way, or about selecting the nominee in the best possible way? Are we concerned, that is, over *who* is nominated or *how* it is accomplished? It is, in short, apparently a conflict over process versus outcome, but as we shall see, it is actually a conflict over power and result.

THE TWO VIEWS OF THE PRESIDENCY

The two views of the presidency rest on values that are important claims and legitimate desires to hold. That is why, of course, that when they do conflict (that is, when their logical incompatibility is realized), the conflict can be so real and important. It is also why it is so difficult, indeed likely impossible, to resolve.

One view, recall, is of the president as a manager, that is as a chief executive and administrator, responsible for a smoothly running government. The president, in this view, is responsible not just for efficiency but for the achievement of consensual values. These latter, as Ostrom and Simon (1985) remind us, are summarized under the three great goals of "peace, prosperity, and tranquility."

The second view is of a president as political leader, as chief agenda setter and as the chief decision maker about where the nation is to go in political and policy terms. Here, the president is the one person most responsible for resolving and, often, choosing, one side over the other (if not creating one of the sides in the first place) in political conflicts and divisions. In this view, the president receives (or at least, under appropriate conditions, may receive) a popular mandate through election and attempts to get the Congress to implement it.

These two differing views run deeply through many aspects of our understanding of the presidency. At one level, for example, two alternative views of voting are held by the public. The president-as-manager point of view lends itself naturally to seeing voting as based on retrospective evaluations (for example, Fiorina 1981). In this view, voters ask whether the president has done a good, effective job. Has he managed to move the world in a peaceful direction, and, in the area most commonly analayzed, has he managed the economy effectively? Retrospective evaluations, therefore, are the voting analogue to the numerous studies of the determinants of presidential approval ratings (for example, Mueller 1973; Ostrom and Simon 1985). Not only may voters ask such questions in framing their decision problem, but so, too, may the candidates seek to campaign on such terms, especially a popular incumbent seeking reelection. Reagan in 1984, much like Eisenhower in 1956 and Nixon in 1972, provides a clear example (see Aldrich and Weko 1987, for details). On the other hand, the president-as-policymaker point of view leads to an idea of electoral choice that is based on comparative assessments along divisive lines such as party, policy, and/or ideology. Does one want a Democrat or Republican, or a liberal or conservative president? Needless to say, candidates at times also seek to frame the voters' choice in such terms. Thus, Reagan in 1980 not only criticized Carter's handling of the presidency, but he proposed a clearly defined set of alternative policy positions. As several have argued (Aldrich and Weko 1987; Hargrove and Nelson 1985; Jacobson 1985), presentation of alternative policy choices in 1980 not only helped define the voters' choice problem, but also defined the policy agenda in Congress, summarized as the "Reagan revolution."

These two views, moreover, reveal themselves even more deeply than in presidential elections and governance. These two views are very similar to the distinction, such as that made by Riker (1982) between a Madisonian, liberal view of democracy and a populist view of democracy. In the first case, the public chooses officeholders and returns them to office or turns them out based on their handling of government. In the second case, the public chooses officeholders because of the policy positions they represent. At the deeper level, of course, these two types of democratic theory differ over the nature of the relationship between the governor and the government, over the purpose of representation and, indeed, over the very idea of democracy.

How, then, do these distinctive views reveal themselves in conflict over nomination processes? The Hamiltonian perspective with which this paper began is one. If the nation is to choose the most efficient and effective manager, what is most important is to have those with the greatest information and understanding of government and, most especially, the set of potential candidates to do the choosing. After all, the central question is competence. If there is little disagreement over ends, if all desire peace, prosperity, and tranquility, what is most at issue is who can best achieve those shared ends. What that means is that, to use John Adams's phrase, the "most wise and good" should choose, for they are in the best position to know who will make the best "magistrate who was to have so important an agency in the administration of the government." Or, in Russell Baker's phrase (1987), it is political leaders not the public who "know who can cut the mustard."

If, however, the problem is to select a president as political leader, and if, most importantly, there are deep political cleavages, the choice is not one of "mere" competency. It is, instead, a choice of policy directions, fought over the selection of individuals with differing alternatives, rather than as individuals with differing qualifications and competencies. To concede influence over the choice to others is to risk folly, for those others may have quite different goals. This is especially so when granting others the power to choose institutionally, that is for some unspecified period (and because they hold particular positions), for, over time, there is no guarantee that that power, once conceded, will be exercised in your interests. Indeed, the granting of power to elites, however defined, is to risk tyranny, quite in the Madisonian sense (for example, *Federalist* No. 10, 1961).

It might be argued that, at least with the great extent of media coverage of both presidential selection and national governance today, we should be in a position to let the people choose. If there is consensus over ends and great volumes of information, the public can choose the most efficient manager. Perhaps in earlier eras there was too little information available to expect the public to choose wisely, but today this is no longer so. And, of course, if there are disagreements over ends, for example a choice between traditional, New Deal democracy, à la Mondale, or a new direction for the party, à la Hart in 1984, the choice ought to be made by the widest possible definition of "Democrats," presumably those in the public sufficiently motivated to vote in the party's primaries. To give such power instead to elites, such as the Democratic political leadership, is to bias the choice toward the traditional, in the direction, that is, that got the leadership to power in the first place. After all, it appears that one definition of such leadership in 1984, the "super delegates" to the 1984 Democratic national convention, overwhelmingly backed one of their own—Mondale —and might have provided just enough votes to put him "over the top" before the 1984 convention opened (see, for example, Abramson, Aldrich, and Rohde 1987).

The problem with this argument highlights today's version of the conflicting values. Information might be available, but the public does not hold it and/or use it in their choices. That, at least, is the position advanced by Baker (1987; he points to television as the culprit), as a representative (of sorts) of "informed opinion." But it is also the view of many academics. In what is perhaps the most extensive analysis of public opinion about presidential nomination choices to date, Keeter and Zukin (1983) title their book, revealingly, *Uninformed Choice,* and claim they toyed with the title "Random Selection."

Today's conflict serves only as an example. As noted earlier, presidential nomination systems have been refined and, more importantly, massively changed with a frequency not found in other arenas. America, with its great compromising governmental system, simply seems unable to strike the right compromise over process—how best to select—and outcome—who best to select.

The fundamental reason that institutional tinkering fails to come up with just the right compromise over process and outcome is that the distinction is *not* really between process and outcome, but a disagreement or conflict between two different types of outcomes. Historically, nomination systems collapse because of this conflict, the conflict over manager versus policymaker. And, try as we might, the problem is that we all want both. We want a smoothly functioning democracy, and thus an able, competent manager. But, if the president is effective, but effective at pursuing ends we find inimical, we want to—and indeed should want to —replace him with one whose ends we do not find inimical, even if that means accepting one who is a bit more of a bumbler. But, then, when one who is a bit of a bumbler turns out to be thoroughly incompetent, we switch our desires—and indeed, if unfortunately, we should. It is not that we are inconsistent or fickle, it is simply that we want too much. We want two values that are not always compatible.

The central argument lodged against placing selection power in the hands of the most well informed is that it is by no means certain that they will hold the value positions of those who grant them that power and, in general, of the populace. This is not a problem if one holds the view that what we want and expect of our president is competence, the managerial virtues. But, it does matter a great deal if one views presidential selection as a choice between alternative values and visions of society for the next four or eight years.

Indeed, nomination systems that have been designed under the managerial vision have been attacked as elite oligarchies, unresponsive to the interests and values of a larger body politic. And, this is often with good cause, as we will see.

Of course, the claim—backed up with much solid, empirical support

—that today's system approximates "random" or at least ill-informed selection is a powerful one, as well. And thus the conflict is joined. Since, however, the process began with a system that emphasized the managerial very heavily and since reforms have been a step-by-step opening of the system to an increasingly broader array of participants, the struggle has proceeded in one particular direction. Only recently have claims been made to reverse the direction. Yet the problem is quite general. To see the nature of this conflict, we must review the sordid history of presidential nomination systems.

PRESIDENTIAL NOMINATION SYSTEMS

We can classify the variety of ways presidents have been nominated into six historical periods, each with its own nomination method.

1. A Deliberative Electoral College

At the Founding, presidential appointment did not recognize nomination and election as separate actions. The original intention was that the eligible citizens of the various states would elect members to the electoral college. The Electors would, in effect, nominate and elect a president at the same time. Only the first election, in 1789, can be considered to have been completely in line with those intentions. The consensus for Washington was obvious—and illustrative of smooth functioning possible under the managerial viewpoint, as long as that consensus could be sustained. By 1792, the Federalist and Democratic-Republican parties were beginning to emerge, and a group of D-R's met formally to challenge the reelection of Adams as vice-president (endorsing New York Governor George Clinton over New York Governor Aaron Burr). By 1796, the congressional caucus was beginning to appear, it was used by both sides in 1800, aided in 1804 by the passage of the Twelfth Amendment, and was open and formal (at least on the D-R side) by 1808.

While it lived a short life as an independent, deliberative body, and while it did so only as long as there was little controversy over who it should be expected to (and did) choose, it is worth examining the arguments for the electoral college. The framing of the electoral college seems to have been relatively uncontroversial. The anti-Federalist opposition to the Constitution, for instance, focused on other matters. According to Storing (1981, p. 49), "Many Anti-Federalists thought that a unitary executive was necessary, for the sake of both efficiency and responsibility, and agreed with The Federal Farmer that the office of the President and the mode of his election were well conceived" (clearly a managerial view of the presidency). As a result, we have relatively little guidance about the purposes the framers saw the electoral college fulfilling. Commentary on it in *The Federalist Papers* for example, is limited to Hamilton's No. 68.

Hamilton listed five arguments in support of the electoral college in *Federalist* No. 68 (1961, pp. 412–13). While he did not suggest that some of these five are more important than others, one can only presume that the order of presentation was intentional.

1. The first argument is that the college should be elected by the people for the express purpose of appointing the president and vice-president. The college thus rests on the principles of a republican democracy, and it would have been, at the very least, impolitic to consider this feature anything but the most important.

2. The second argument is more important for our purposes, as it outlines the central reason for making the election indirectly dependent on popular vote. It is worth quoting in its entirety:

> It was equally desirable that the immediate election should be made by men most capable of analyzing the qualities adapted to the station and acting under circumstances favorable to deliberation, and to a judicious combination of all the reasons and inducements which were proper to govern their choice. A small number of persons, selected by their fellow-citizens from the general mass, will be most likely to possess the information and discernment requisite to so complicated an investigation. (1961, p. 412)

In other words, the basic notion was that the people could discern a set of what Sorauf (1976, p. 268) refers to as "respected notables," but only these notables could be assumed to have the *information* and *discernment* to be capable of deciding the complicated matter of who would be the best president.

3. The third argument concerns the necessity of avoiding "tumult and disorder." The choice of the electors would be less likely "to convulse

the community" than would the community's direct election of the president.

4. The electors were to be kept, insofar as institutional arrangements could guarantee, from "cabal, intrigue, and corruption." The transient life of the body, as well as the thirteen separate meeting places, would help keep them from that exposure. But the requirement that "no senator, representative, or other person holding a place of trust or profit under the United States can be of the number of the electors" would mean they would begin their deliberation "free from any sinister bias."

5. This last requirement provides another mechanism (besides the reformulation of the college each four years) for achieving the fifth goal; that the president be beholden for his office to no one (or at least no known set of individuals) other than the public as a whole.

In sum, point one is the basis of democratic principles for selecting the president. The second point concerns the republican principle; that only "the most wise and good" are capable of making such a crucial decision, while points three through five are that they should do so in as independent and dispassionate a way as possible, free from corruption, free from intrigue, and free from organized politicking as we know it. In short, it is to be a representative, democratic selection, but one ideally geared to have a mangerial president "above politics" and independent of politics.

As I noted, a deliberative college failed as soon as organized political parties arose. With organization came the possibility—one quickly seized —that candidates for electors would run on party slates, and as slates promising to support a particular candidate for president. The effects, then, were to destroy the deliberativeness of the electoral college, and to make the election of the president as nearly directly dependent upon popular will as possible. However, to have a slate pledged to support a particular presidential hopeful requires some method of choosing that hopeful. The initial mechanism was the congressional caucus.

2. King Caucus

The D-R party, in particular, quickly resolved the dilemma of coordinating electors by having its members in the house caucus to select the party nominee. The congressional caucus has some similarities to the ideal-type

John H. Aldrich

electoral college. Its members were elected directly by the people, sepa-
rately in the various states. It was a fairly small group who were, arguably,
"respected notables." It differs from the college in several important ways.
The caucus was not transient and selected in a timely fashion for the
exclusive purpose of appointing presidential nominees. Obviously, they
were officeholders, holding a "place of trust" and "profit." They met
regularly and in a single place. They could not be guaranteed to be free
from "cabal, intrigue, and corruption," nor "from any sinister bias." They
well might be exposed to "heats and ferments," and the president might
be nearly as beholden for reelection as is a prime minister. Obviously, the
caucus could emerge only once there were existing, organized, and influential party structures in the United States. In short, what is left of
Hamilton's five arguments are points one and two. The remaining defense, therefore, is of election, but an indirect one where nominations are
decided by those most informed and capable. Thus the caucus represents
the first compromise between managerial efficiency on the one hand and
party political imperatives on the other.

Whether congressional caucus nominations would have led to great
influence over an incumbent president, or even an aspiring hopeful, we
shall never know, for the congressional caucus lasted only from 1800 or so
to 1824. The members of the caucus were, as members of Congress of the
same party, united by common interest. Whether from Madison on tyranny or Michels on the iron law of oligarchy, we would anticipate that it
would be only a matter of time until the common interest would conflict
with the rights of other citizens or with the permanent and aggregate
interests of the community—that is, be what Madison called a faction.
This potential became even more salient with the demise of the Federalist
party. By 1816, nomination from the D-R party was tantamount to election. And, by 1824, many saw the caucus as a faction.

The problem was simply that the D-R's congressional caucus was seen
not just as having too much power, but also as using it arbitrarily and
capriciously. In particular, large segments felt their interests were not
represented fully in "King Caucus." This would not matter under a
managerial view, based as it is on a presumed consensus on ends, namely
nonpolitical efficiency, but it matters greatly under a political imperative
assumption. In fact, only a relatively few D-R members of Congress
attended the caucus of 1824—three-quarters coming from Georgia, New
York, North Carolina, and Virginia all on the seaboard (*Guide to U.S.*

Elections 1985, p. 11). Three main opponents to the caucus's nominee, Secretary of the Treasury William H. Crawford, remained viable presidential candidates (Secretary of State John Quincy Adams, House Speaker Henry Clay, and Senator Andrew Jackson). Their viability rested on a different form of nomination; nomination by state legislatures. The presumption was that, while the members of "King Caucus" might have had the information and discernment to select wise and just leaders, they were not fulfilling this capability. They were no longer representative of the party as a whole, and they, therefore, lost their legitimacy. The question was not whether Crawford would make a good administrator, the question was whether his *policy* goals reflected those of large segments of the party.

3. State Legislative Caucuses

Nomination by state legislatures has something of a compromise quality to it. Presumably, letting each state have the potential to nominate a candidate would open up the party and include representation of a wide variety of viewpoints. It would go back to the electoral college in the sense of having separate meeting places, and state legislatures presumably could wield lesser influence over a nominee or incumbent than the caucus in Congress. It would mean some sacrifice of immediate contact with potential nominees and the problems they would face; that is, it would have lesser relevant information. But, it would remain true to the republican principle (and, presumably, state legislators are close to "respected notables"). It would also be true to the democratic principle and be less open to "sinister bias" (or, perhaps, it would, in the aggregate, "sum over" individual idiosyncracies of "cabal and intrigue" and "sinister bias"). The central problem, of course, was that it was too unwieldy and cumber- some a process. *Too many* people could be nominated. The irony was, of course, that the four nominees of 1824 led to an indecisive electoral college and decision in the House of Representatives—the very body that was, in the one-party system, too arbitrary as "King Caucus," too much an elite oligarchy. Perhaps not surprisingly, the 1824 election was resolved apparently by the so-called "corrupt bargain" (Adams possibly exchanging the position of secretary of state, the then usual stepping stone to the presidency, for Clay's support).

4. Political Party Conventions

State legislatures again nominated presidential candidates in 1828. Jackson and Adams were nominated by several legislatures, and only these two were so nominated. Nonetheless, the potential for a widely split party, the beginnings of organized opposition to the D-R party, namely the Whig party, and the invention of the national party convention by the Anti-Mason party in 1831, led to the adoption of a national party convention for the purpose of nominating a presidential candidate, *inter alia*, by all major parties. This invention, of course, remains to this day.

The idea of a political party convention is that all interests of the party can be represented at its national meetings. It is in some ways a reversion to the electoral college. All states can choose their members for the nearly exclusive purpose of selecting nominees. It is a transient body. While it does meet in one place, it would seem relatively less open to "sinister bias," but of course could be swept in that place by "heats and ferments," such as with William Jennings Bryan's "Cross of Gold" speech at the 1896 Democratic convention. The body itself has the potential for "tumult and disorder"; indeed they seem endemic. Organized demonstrations and silly hats do not seem consonant with "calm, dispassionate, reflective judgement," but the mass body on the floor of the convention rarely was where the real judgments were passed anyway. Convention delegates may be somewhat less obviously "respected notables" than the ideal elector, but they remain to this day quite distinctive from the general public on key dimensions, including political information, experience, and knowledge. And, of course, many are indeed "respected notables."

Thus, the national party convention struck a different sort of compromise; one that was more broadly representative of national party opinion than, say, "King Caucus," and yet one that yielded as delegates people among those most likely to have the requisite political information and discernment to make wise choices. Not surprisingly, then, it was not only accepted as a reasonable basis for selecting nominees, but it also withstood the test of time. There was no serious challenge to it as a legitimate institution for seventy years, it remains the legitimating body today, and many current reforms add up to calls to reinstate some of its actual power lost over the last seventy years. Its strength as compromise was that its decisions were to be made by well-informed political leaders, but leaders found throughout the nation, and thus presumably reflecting the diversity of political opinion in the party as a whole.

5. The Progressive Era and the Primaries

If "King Caucus" was derided as an elite oligarchy and that decision led to the development and acceptance of the national convention, then history repeated itself around the turn of the twentieth century. Political parties were under attack by progressives, among others, as elite oligarchies. Not only were they seen as political elites but, once again, they were seen as arbitrarily and capriciously using their power. They were no longer seen by all as broadly representative of popular opinion, and indeed opposition took the route of attacking not just the men in power but the mechanisms they used to attain and to hold that power. The opposition was focused, of course, on the local party organization more than on the national party "organization," such as it was. Machines, it was argued, had shut out far too many from the party base (especially the growing middle class), and one of many of the institutions manipulated for the machine's own ends was the nomination system. For the first time, there was a serious attempt to make nominations as close as possible to a direct election, one dependent directly on the expressed opinion of the general public.

The argument was that the party convention system for nominating candidates was no longer true to the republican principle. Those who were effective in choosing nominees certainly were not chosen by the people to perform that task. But, the argument went further by claiming that the formal party organizations had closed themselves off from the influence of the public except through the most circuitous and limited of indirect means; too limited and too circuitous to remain consistent with the republican principle. Moreover, the bosses, it was argued, had developed an extensive variety of formal and informal institutional mechanisms to insulate themselves from popular opinion and to retain their power. A major set of mechanisms aimed at these presumably tyrannical ends (tyrannical at least in the sense of Madison, that is of "adverse . . . to the permanent and aggregate interests of the community," *Federalist*, 1961, p. 78) was the variety of means used to control party nominations. As was the case with the attack on "King Caucus," it is not coincidental that nomination for offices controlled by the machine was tantamount to election in these virtually one-party locales. The point was, of course, that widely shared policy viewpoints were being excluded systematically from representation and, thus, from influence.

To "open up the system" to popular control, Progressives proposed for the first time the essential abolition of the republican principle in nominations. The primary was designed to make nomination to office a direct election. It need hardly be said that Progressives believed not only that different sorts of candidates would be nominated (for example, not just "party hacks") but also that they, the Progressives, would benefit either by being more viable themselves or, at least, by seeing progressive principles receive greater attention by more, and more successful, candidates.

The primary was advocated for all elective offices and indeed the presidential primary was the result more of a spillover from other primaries than of a subject of central concern in and of itself. Moreover, there was by no means unanimity over the abandonment of the republican principle in presidential nominations. First, there was no serious effort to eliminate national party conventions. Secondly, even though many states adopted presidential primaries by, say, 1916, more did not. Thirdly, some presidential primaries remained true to republicanism in the sense that people could express a preference only for who would be their delegates to the convention. Other primaries were of the type that permitted the expression of presidential preference, presumably providing delegates actually selected via caucus or primary vote with information about candidate sentiment. That information could be ignored at the delegates' pleasure in many cases.

The presumptions underlying presidential primaries are twofold. First, any legally eligible candidate can present his or her case to the public, even if that means "going over the heads of the party to the people." Second, any legally eligible citizen can have a direct say in the nomination process, either by helping select delegates or by helping to instruct them (even legally binding them) on how to vote at the convention.

Even at the high-water mark for this hybrid convention-primary system, neither presumption worked. Until 1972 with George McGovern, no candidate who ran against the party by going "over their heads" to the public was successful. Casual examination suggests that the correlation between the votes received in primaries and the vote received on the convention floor would be very large and negative. That such a popular and politically influential candidate as Theodore Roosevelt could run so strongly in his public campaign and lose decisively at the convention dramatically illustrates the point. In short, public input to the nomination system remained severely limited, especially in comparison to its impact in nominations for such as governorships and Congress. There, the primary was widely accepted and became a mechanism for direct selection by the eligible and voting public.

6. Recent Reforms

In part because of increased media attention, presidential primaries began to assume a somewhat greater role in nominations after World War II. By 1960, for example, John Kennedy saw primary victories as a necessary condition for receiving the nomination. But he used them to demonstrate that potential liabilities (for example, youth, inexperience, and his Catholic faith) would not be insurmountable obstacles in a general election campaign. In effect, he used his victories in the Wisconsin and West Virginia primaries, among others, as bargaining chips to encourage party leaders such as Chicago Mayor Richard Daley to support his candidacy. While a successful primary campaign may have been a necessary condition for his nomination, it was far from a sufficient condition. Four years later, Senator Barry Goldwater probably needed his single primary victory in California to win the Republican nomination, but delegates won in primary campaigns were, once again, but a minority of his support. Put alternatively, had all states used primaries as decisive in selecting, or instructing delegates, Goldwater almost certainly would have lost, and, if a single national primary had been used, a Goldwater victory would have been almost inconceivable.

A country that had gotten used to having some role in nomination contests by 1968 and one that was beset by major divisions that year could be expected to have a core of vocal opposition to a nomination process in which a nominee could be selected without conducting a formal public campaign. Hubert Humphrey won the Democratic party nomination in 1968 in a classic instance of the suggested negative correlation between primary votes and convention support. Anti-Johnson and antiwar activists could choose between Senators Eugene McCarthy and Robert Kennedy in several presidential primaries, but they could not receive the pleasure of voting against the administration after the New Hampshire primary; and yet the remaining administration candidate won nomination easily.

The Democratic convention in Chicago in 1968 was certainly a nominating body deciding in "tumult and disorder," full of "heats and disorders," which, at least to some in the community was seen as "convulsing" it with "extraordinary and violent movements." Too many well-placed Democrats saw the convention deciding under the influence of "cabal, intrigue, and corruption" and perhaps tainted with "sinister bias." The problem was, of course, that the process by which Humphrey succeeded in winning the nomination was seen as too much in the hands of the organized party and its leaders and too little open to the influence of public opinion. The irony is that the Goldwater nomination illustrated the degree to which loyal followers of a candidate could penetrate the established party and that, in general, the party as formal organization and as electoral touchstone was perceived to be in serious decline. The reform efforts initiated at and after the Chicago convention succeeded in doing what the Progressive era reform efforts had failed to achieve; the formal "elite oligarchy" of organized party members was destroyed. Humphrey's nomination was the death knell of the national nominating conventions as deliberative bodies introduced 157 years earlier.

The problem once again was not just that the "respected notables" or delegates were an elite different from the public as a whole, but that they had used their power in an apparently arbitrary and capricious way to thwart the wishes of the public as expressed, apparently, in that year's presidential primaries. (One might well wonder how electoral history would have been had Humphrey defeated his opponents in primary elections that year.) The subsequent reforms, therefore, were designed to open up the system to larger numbers of candidates and to provide a more nearly decisive role for the public in affecting their party's presidential nominations.

Where the Progressive era reforms failed, the Democratic reforms of the 1960s and 1970s succeeded. First, large numbers of candidates run (at least in the absence of an incumbent seeking renomination), and the successes of McGovern and Carter (1976) and near successes of such as Bush, Anderson, and Hart suggest the potential for victory that might be perceived by candidates who would not have believed they had much hope at all in the system used through 1968. Secondly, a much larger proportion of the general public do participate in the thirty and more primaries of the current era than participated in any earlier era. Many more could participate if they choose, but any argument that primary voters are an "elite oligarchy" would be almost laughably ineffective.

Thirdly, the results of the primary and more open caucus proceedings of today have been decisive in every case so far, and there is reason to believe that the voters in primaries and "voters" in caucuses will be decisive ordinarily (see Aldrich 1980). In short, the public's actions are decisive. Convention delegates *could*, of course, play a decisive role but the chances are very good that, in terms of selecting presidential nominees, their role ordinarily will be little more independent than, say, a present-day member of the electoral college. In fact, the debate in the 1980 Democratic convention over the so-called "open convention" rule was over whether a delegate had the freedom to choose independently or whether he or she was as bound to have no more independent power over the presidential nomination than an elector does over the selection of the president. And, the "open convention" rule lost.

What I believe this description adds up to is this: the reform efforts that have succeeded have shared several characteristics. First, they have been most centrally concerned about "opening up" the system; always to more active decision makers and generally to more potential nominees. But, that is to say that each successful reform has been concerned most centrally with *process*, how best to nominate a candidate. Secondly, as far as I can tell, there has never been any serious questioning of the importance of having those central to the decision-making process possess as much relevant information as possible. In fact, the reforms have all represented fairly short steps toward, say, participation by the general public; only gradually have we come to play that central role. I take this fact as evidence that there has been considerable doubt about the sufficiency of information in the public. Thirdly, however, is the recognition that, while possession of requisite information may be necessary to making wise choices, it certainly is *not* sufficient. In fact, most episodes of change were successful precisely because there was a sufficiently widely shared perception that mere possession of information was insufficient. The well-informed had used their power over nominations in a way seen as arbitrary and capricious.

In sum, then, the structural changes in our method of nominating presidents have been a fairly consistent move toward making presidential nominations an increasingly more direct form of election. The decisive, independent, and deliberative power has moved from a rather small number of individuals to an ever larger number. It is certainly not now a complete, direct election system (as would be a single national primary over presidential contenders with, say, the plurality winner receiving the nomination). But, the current system is a much closer approximation of a direct election than the electoral college, the congressional caucus, or a machine-dominated convention. The direct expression of candidate preference by the general public has been decisive in all nomination campaigns since 1968, in which the current system has been used in one form or another. We have, in short, a close approximation of a directly democratic system, but we have moved very far from a republican system. Delegates may be elected or appointed, but too many of them are also instructed by the public of their various states to allow room for independent judgment to matter.

The central question, then, is this: while we have a system consistent with Hamilton's first point in defense of the electoral college, do we have a system consistent with his second point: Is the public in a position "to possess the information and discernment requisite to so complicated an investigation"? While the question is as yet incompletely answered, available evidence suggests either that the answer is no (for example, Keeter and Zukin 1983), or, if possibly yes, a yes that comes only very late in the campaign, well after most candidates have been eliminated and dynamics and "horse race" aspects of the campaign have greatly shaped its course (see Bartels 1987; Aldrich and Rahn 1987).

SHOULD WE REFORM THE SYSTEM?

The argument I have made is that the (episodic) evolution of our methods of nominating presidential candidates has moved monotonically from the electoral college to the current system, but that movement has been across two continua simultaneously. By, at each step, enlarging the set of relevant decision makers, we have made our nomination process more and more nearly an approximation of direct democracy and even the representational-type reforms were justified by providing a better, more accurate representation of general party sentiment. At the same time, however, we have made a necessary condition for "wise choices," namely possession of relevant information, successively more problematic. And, I believe that movement has been across these two dimensions precisely because they are *almost* necessarily joined—negatively. What we have now is not the most extreme point on the continuum; a one-day national primary that is decisive would be at least a bit more so. But, we are obviously closer to it today than at any other time in U.S. history.

What I argue about our current system is that it is paradoxical with respect to information. For all but the more inattentive, there is at least a sufficient amount of information fairly readily available in the mass media by, say, June (at least, I believe it is a reasonable coverage, taken as a whole, even if it contains a lot of irrelevancies—see Aldrich 1980; Aldrich and Rahn 1987). Of course, for those quite attentive, there is a lot of information available, especially on policy if not leadership ability, and the information is available rather early. For all but these two extremes, however, the availability of a reasonable amount of information is limited in two ways. First, for many candidates, and historically for a large majority of candidates contesting for the out-party nomination, there is never a "lot" of information about them in the easy-access, public domain, and the diversity that only develops over the course of the campaign by contesting in various locales is absent. These candidates never really had a significant chance of winning nomination (or, alternatively, which one of them does win their party nomination, whether McGovern, Carter, Bush, or Hart, hinges, perhaps, on the luck of winning but a few more votes). Secondly, while citizens can (and I suspect do) learn a fair amount about the few primary campaigns with longevity, the requisite information accumulates in the easy-access public domain too late to make a difference.

What, then, about possible reforms? The central point is that reforms ought to be addressed seriously to the dual, information-process continua. Consider, for example, the sort of reform enacted by the Hunt Commission in the Democratic party, for the 1984 convention—the reservation of some delegate slots for party notables who would be selected as uncommitted. The intention of such reforms (or as Hunt called them "disreforms") has been expressed by columnist and former editorial page editor of the *Washington Star* Edwin M. Yoder, Jr. *(Minneapolis Tribune*, January 25, 1982; p. 8A):

> Almost everyone seems to agree now that both parties would produce more appealing nominees if political peers were more influential in the selection process. There are things to be learned that cannot be gleaned from the deceptive devices of television or the frivolous clamor of primary campaigning.
>
> Oddly, the great reform spasm of the Democratic Party produced an enhanced appearance of representativeness but less of the thing itself. This clearly had something to do with the banishment of elected offi-

cials. Common sense suggests that they, having met the test of public
approval, might know a bit about the voters. . . . And who was replac-
ing them? Local activists, by and large, who were by income, education
and attitude atypical of American voters: an elite in fact.

Clearly, the central point of Yoder's argument is that the public does not
have the same extent of pertinent information—and the delegates they
now select may not either. That the new breed of delegates are an "elite"
is irrelevant for two reasons. First, elected officials, "by and large, were"
and are "by income, education and attitude atypical of American voters:
an elite, in fact." But it is more fundamental that, under our current
system, the identity of delegates is practically irrelevant in the selection of
nominees. We, the public, do not select representatives, we select nominees.

So, if the "disreform" were to be effective, it would have to mean that,
at least on occasion, the delegates would select a nominee who was *not*
the "winner" of the primary season. Only then would representation
matter. If that were to happen, I suspect that we would hit upon the same
problem that has characterized prior reforms. Information may be necessary but it is not a sufficient condition for making wise choices. Would
not the "winner" of the primary season but the loser of the nomination
be in a similar circumstance to, say, a McCarthy in 1968? Would not his
supporters be in a rather strong position to argue that the representatives
might have had the information but nonetheless used their power arbitrarily and capriciously? And, having once had the central role in nominations, would not the public be particularly susceptible to such appeals?
Now, I am not saying that some such disreform is bad (or good). Instead,
what I am saying is that serious attention needs to be given to both sides
of the dilemma: democratic process and good outcomes (including that
information is necessary but not sufficient for making wise choices).

Or, consider the idea of a national primary. This proposal has the
merits of process and, indeed, its results may be accepted as legitimate
just as primary elections for other offices are so accepted. It, however,
would put the greatest premium on information. It is difficult to predict
how the national media would cover such events and thus what sorts and
amounts of information would fall into the "easy-access, public domain."
But, it certainly seems reasonable to suggest that the already well-known
candidate would be significantly advantaged—as he (and, possibly some-
day soon, she) already is. But, in addition, it seems rather unlikely that

any little-known challengers would arise in the same fashion as the system of today permits. Of course, one set of arguments for a national primary is precisely that it would make it difficult for candidates like McGovern and Carter to succeed. But, the important point is that the already well-known candidates are advantaged *regardless* of their policy or other characteristics. They are advantaged simply because they are well known. This point is another way of saying that information is necessary for wise choices, but it is not sufficient.

On the other hand, Hamilton's justifications for the electoral college, after the points about democracy and trustee-type representations, are concerned. It seems to me, with attempting to reduce the possibility of the misuse of power (free from "sinister biases," "heats and ferments," and so forth). The only check, however, was the hope of a dispassionate elector. Historically, the only institutional check I can think of is "prior restraint." As electors have run for election already committed (in principle and, for many states, in legal fact), so many delegates have run their public campaigns committed by principle/personal preference or by law (and often both) as supporters of a particular presidential candidate. It is very difficult to imagine another reasonable, nonextreme case, check on the arbitrary and capricious use of power vested in some sort of representative-based nomination system. And, as I have indicated already, I believe that the apparent impossibility has led to the asymmetries in the various reform struggles and the so far consistent movement toward process over outcome.

The above may sound like an argument for a democratic process-type solution with perhaps some institutional mechanisms for generating substantial, systematic, timely, and easy-access information. There is a final complication. The Founders, it seems to me, were less concerned with, say, the platforms of various presidential candidates and with selection of the candidate offering the better platform. Rather, they were concerned more with the qualifications and competencies of the individual candidates. William Riker makes this argument (1982) and argues even more strenuously that elections can*not* serve to express the public sentiment on policy, but can only select the best leader (or vote out an undesirable incumbent). The problem is that a candidate's platform is a reasonably straightforward factual matter (with the exceptions of purposeful deception, genuine change, or the complexities of many issues). Providing information about competency and leadership qualities is much less straightforward. Most of such "information" consists of the factual aspects of prior experience, and so forth, and of the less factual aspects of intention, goals, and other hopes. The real advantage of, say, the congressional caucus was that many of its members were likely to have had extensive personal contact with most of the candidates; a much more immediate and experiential "measure of the man" could be made. In short, it may be much easier to manipulate the amount of nearly factual information available to the public (for example, policy positions) than the amount or quality of judgmental information, especially since there is no agreement on what makes leaders good, let alone great.

Thus, I can only conclude that it may not be possible to strike a compromise between the selection of the best president as manager and the preferred president as policymaker. They are both valuable and cherished aspirations, but they are, simply, logically incompatible. As a result, there is no institution that can guarantee that they will not on occasion conflict—and, unfortunately, when they do conflict, it is an occasion of great moment. Man, simply, cannot create that which is logically impossible.

REFERENCES

Abramson, Paul R., John H. Aldrich, and David W. Rohde (1987). *Change and Continuity in the 1984 Elections,* rev. ed. (Washington, D.C.: CQ Press).

Aldrich, John H. (1980). *Before the Convention: Strategies and Choices in Presidential Nomination Campaigns* (Chicago: University of Chicago Press).

Aldrich, John H., and Wendy Rahn (1987). "The Dynamics of Candidate Support in Presidential Nomination Campaigns: The Development of Support for Gary Hart in 1984," unpublished mimeograph, Department of Political Science, University of Minnesota.

Aldrich, John H., and Thomas Weko (1987). "The Presidency and the Elections Process: Campaign Strategy, Voting, and Governance," in Michael Nelson, ed., *The Presidency and the Political System,* 2d ed. (Washington, D.C.: CQ Press).

Baker, Russell (1987). "All Lose in Presidential Game Show," *Minneapolis Star and Tribune,* March 16, p. 12A.

Bartels, Larry M. (1987). "Candidate Choice and the Dynamics of the Presidential Nomination Process," *American Journal of Political Science* 31, February, pp. 1–30.

The Federalist Papers. See Hamilton, Alexander, James Madison, and John Jay.

Fiorina, Morris P. (1981). *Retrospective Voting in American National Elections* (New Haven: Yale University Press).

Guide to U.S. Elections, 2d ed. (1985) (Washington, D.C.: Congressional Quarterly).

Hamilton, Alexander, James Madison, and John Jay ([1787–88] 1961). *The Federalist Papers,* edited by Clinton Rossiter (New York: New American Library).

Hargrove, Erwin C., and Michael Nelson (1985). "The Presidency: Reagan and the Cycle of Politics and Policy," in Michael Nelson, ed., *The Elections of 1984* (Washington, D.C.: CQ Press).

Jacobson, Gary C. (1985). "Congress: Politics After a Landslide Without Coattails," in Michael Nelson, ed., *The Elections of 1984* (Washington, D.C.: CQ Press).

Keeter, Scott, and Cliff Zukin (1983). *Uninformed Choice: The Failure of the New Nominating System* (New York: Praeger).

Mueller, John E. (1973). *War, Presidents and Public Opinion* (New York: John Wiley).

Ostrom, Charles W., Jr., and Dennis M. Simon (1985). "Promise and Performance: A Dynamic Model of Presidential Popularity," *American Political Science Review* 79, June, pp. 334–58.

Riker, William H. (1982). *Liberalism Against Populism: A Confrontation Between the Theory of Democracy and the Theory of Social Choice* (San Francisco: W. H. Freeman).

Sorauf, Frank J. (1976). *Party Politics in America,* 3rd ed. (Boston: Little, Brown).

Storing, Herbert J. (1981). *What the Anti-Federalists Were For* (Chicago: University of Chicago Press).

Yoder, Edwin M., Jr. (1982). "Disreforming the Democratic Party," *Minneapolis Tribune,* January 25, p. 8A.

III

PRESIDENTIAL IMAGE IN AMERICAN POLITICS

LOOKING PRESIDENTIAL is what candidates often strive to project in their campaigns and to sustain while in office. News media coverage offers presidents and presidential hopefuls an opportunity to appear before the nation with official-looking emblems on podiums and American flags at their sides. Political opinion polls ask voters to judge whether candidates are "presidential material." And when presidents are elected, citizens are asked whether they approve of the way the president is handling "his job." We take for granted that presidents and those vying for the office produce images (Greenstein 1965). We know that the media plays an important role in creating these images (Bennett 1983), as well as making them accessible to the public (Barber 1980). Further, social scientists have begun to acknowledge the role of public opinion polls themselves in constructing images of what is considered "presidential behavior." Although we know that images are signifiers of political messages, we do not know very much about the politics of presidential images. This section of the book explores that issue: How do presidents present themselves and what are the political consequences of their symbolic acts?

Long ago, Thurman Arnold noted that political behavior is symbolic of the various characters an actor assumes or plays in the daily dramas of political life. Arnold sought to apply this insight to political institutions, such as courts. He suggested that

> As with individuals, so it is with the institutions which cement groups of individuals together in such a way that they achieve a sort of separate personality. Institutions—whether courts, commercial banks, or government bureaus—develop institutional habits, entirely separable from the personal habits of those who spend their working hours in their service. They build for themselves little dramas, and play varied roles. (1935, p. iv)

Today, the study of symbolic politics focuses on how problems such as poverty, unemployment, and international conflict are continuously constructed and reconstructed by political actors and institutions (Edelman 1988). Students of presidential politics are beginning to apply these insights to the study of the presidency (Hinckley 1987).

In chapter 5, Barbara Hinckley provides a framework for studying presidential images. She is not concerned with how the media or interest groups interpret presidential images, but instead directs us to look at how presidents present themselves. Using the public speeches of presidents

Truman through Reagan, Hinckley identifies consistent patterns of institutional representation that cut across the peculiarity of individual style
and personality and the ideology of political parties. While not all presidents speak to the same audiences or talk on the same topics, Hinckley
finds striking similarities in what they say about the office of the presidency. These are images of the institution, and Hinckley argues that they
establish expectations as well.

Indeed, institutional expectations are a central part of the picture presidents present. Whether or not presidents fulfill the expectations they
associate with the office is not what Hinckley finds most interesting about
this discovery. Instead she suggests that calls for reform, such as those
during the Watergate period, play an important political function by
mediating between the unrealistic expectations presidents present and
their own awareness, as well as the public's, that the White House does
not fulfill these expectations. The continual call for reform is one consequence of symbolic representation. Reforms embrace institutional expectations in their efforts to realize them. Hinckley concludes that reforms
themselves are part of the cult of the presidency.

There are other effects of presidential images. In chapter 6, Nathaniel
Beck examines the relationship between the public and the president as
one of "principal and agent" with regard to elections and the economy.
The electorate, as principal, is assumed to monitor presidential activities
to assess the degree to which they comply with their own preferences.
The electorate, however, must balance these monitoring activities among
a multitude of other potential uses of their time and because of this have
relatively few incentives to formulate sophisticated evaluations of presidential performance. The president, it is assumed, seeks to promote the
economic policies he favors while making sure that he can be reelected.
According to Beck, voters judge the president on a relatively simple basis.
Presidents may take advantage of these simplified judgments by making
economic policy that creates the image of economic prosperity but has
detrimental long-term economic consequences. Beck's analysis alerts us to
economic strategies and resources presidents have to promote positive
images, and the difficulties the electorate has in holding presidents
acountable for their economic policies.

While Beck draws our attention to the interplay of presidential image
and accountability in the domestic realm, Bruce Miroff examines the use
of symbolism and secrecy by presidents in foreign policy. In chapter 7, he
describes a dangerous coexistence of secrecy and high public visibility.

The former conceals what presidents and their aides do, while the latter "mystifies their activities." The Iran-Contra affair provides an excellent example of how presidents try to pursue foreign policies that lack congressional, legal, and popular support. The costs of such hidden schemes are particularly, if not only, high once the cover is blown. However, if presidents are able to employ the doctrine of "plausible deniability," as in this case, they may effectively carry out foreign policies without democratic accountability.

On the other side of the coin is presidential visibility. Here Miroff uses the story of the 1983 invasion of Grenada by U.S. forces to illustrate a presidential spectacle. President Reagan's ratings in the polls increased as the drama of the event progressed from White House pictures of the president mobilized into action; rushed off the golf course, into his bathrobe, and sitting at a meeting with his advisers. Miroff's account of the White House spectacle demonstrates that the most visible foreign policy decisions may hide as much information from the public as those decisions made in secret.

Whether the modern presidency is in fact more secretive is hard to know, in part because of the very nature of secrecy. We might also challenge the proposition that political spectacles are more frequent in the modern presidency; perhaps they are only made more obvious by modern technology. But in either case, Miroff shows the complexity of presidential images, the visible and not so visible ones, in American politics.

REFERENCES

Arnold, Thurman W. (1935). *The Symbols of Government*. New Haven: Yale University Press.

Barber, James David (1980). *The Pulse of Politics: Electing Presidents in the Media Age*. New York: Norton.

Bennett, W. Lance (1983). *News: The Politics of Illusion*. New York: Longman.

Edelman, Murray (1988). *Constructing the Political Spectacles*. Chicago: University of Chicago Press.

Greenstein, Fred I. (1965). "Popular Images of the President," *American Journal of Psychiatry* 122:523.

Hinckley, Barbara (1987). *The Symbolic Presidency*. Chatham, N.J.: Chatham House.

FIVE

Beyond Reform

Barbara Hinckley

Once again the news told us that something was wrong at the White House. Government documents, academic conferences, and media commentators rush to explain what went wrong in the Reagan administration and what should be done to correct it. Thus, commentary in the wake of the Iran-Contra affair joins a time-honored tradition of reform writing. We judge the state of the presidency by the current incumbent in the office, the problems to be corrected by the leading stories of the day.

Reformers in the 1940s and 1960s sought ways to increase the power of the office. Presidents such as FDR or Kennedy could come fresh from a popular election mandate and find their programs blocked by a little band of Supreme Court justices or congressional committee members who had come to office long before. But by the 1970s in contrast, reformers tried to limit the office and make it more accountable. People spoke of the "imperial presidency" and called for ways to check executive excesses. Joining in the spirit, Congress passed the War Powers Act in 1974 and sought changes in budget making and oversight to limit presidential power. Or, to take another example, reformers in the 1950s called for an expanded White House staff and improved organizational machinery to help presidents take control of their own bureaucracy. Then, following Watergate and Vietnam, the new machinery itself became the subject of criticism. Alexander George, Irving Janis, and others called for improvements in the quality, rather than the quantity, of White House decisions. The help itself, and the kind of biases it introduced, became the problem for reform.[1]

This lack of a historical memory is obvious but not surprising. Knowledge about the presidency has lagged behind other American political institutions. Researchers face the difficulty of access to presidents and their advisers, the limited number of cases to generalize about, and the impossibility of knowing what went on behind the closed doors of the Oval Office. Perhaps the greatest obstacle comes from the notion that we already know about the subject. The White House is, by an overwhelming margin, the lead news story of the day.[2] As citizens, people feel they should know about the presidents and have opinions about them. Everyone becomes an expert on this one political subject. So, it is hard to say we do not understand the office that people read and talk about every day.

Despite these difficulties, political scientists have recently given the presidency a new and more rigorous attention. Studies identify the constraints that all presidents face from the ticking of the political clock, economic fluctuations, and the partisan makeup of Congress.[3] Other studies show the similarity of reactions in forming agendas, devising public strategies, and dealing with Congress and interest groups.[4] Presidents are similar to each other in their use of force in limited military engagements, responding more to public attitudes toward war and toward the president than to international effects.[5] This is not to say that individual variations do not exist. But the findings underscore the importance of a historical perspective and the risk of individual-level interpretations.

Institutions can be defined as stable patterns of action and expectations that persist over time, independent of any particular individual or set of circumstances. In his classic account of the subject, Philip Selznik points out the dynamic that lies behind this persistence. Expectations develop over time. They then affect subsequent actions and future expectations.[6] Institutions, then, can be defined by the expectations held about them and will be changed only by changing the expectations. If the presidency is an institution in this sense of the term, then we need to look more closely at these expectations. They should have direct relevance, too, for any autopsies of past events or proposals for change. The expectations themselves may be part of the problem or part of the call for reform.

I have been looking at the presidents' own presentations of the office, using the official record of the *Public Papers*.[7] In major and minor addresses, to a national audience and to smaller groups, presidents make a "presentation of self," to use Erving Goffman's term, that creates a picture of themselves and the government. At one level these statements can be taken as expressions of the presidents' own expectations—what they think a president should say and be. At a second level, they shape the expectations of others: their audience, other people who must interact with that figure that the presidents present; and future generations of citizens and presidents. The presidents say what presidents are expected to be.

The speeches are drawn from all contemporary presidents from Truman through Reagan, using the first three years of each term.[8] Speeches include major addresses broadcast live to a national audience: inaugurals, foreign policy and economic policy speeches, and a sample of State of the Union messages. They also include a sample of minor addresses selected to vary the kind of audience addressed. In minor addresses presidents speak to groups smaller than a nationwide audience. They speak to groups within their own party, groups closely associated with their positions (labor groups for Democratic presidents, for example) and groups associated with the other party's positions (labor groups for Republican presidents, for example).

Of particular interest is the *similarity* of presentation that holds across the years in spite of differences in circumstance or individual style. It is easy to say, well, if the speech writers write the speeches and the advisers set the schedules, where is the president in all this? The point is that to the extent there are similarities beyond the very different speechwriters and advisers, then we can say something about the institution. Something is carrying on—with presidents as diverse as Eisenhower and Kennedy, Nixon and Carter, Truman and Reagan—that is important to see about the office itself.

Several key findings from the larger study[9] have direct relevance here. We can first look at these findings and then turn to the implications for reform.

THE FINDINGS

Three components, among others, are part of a picture of government presented consistently by all presidents, Truman to Reagan. For the first part of the picture, *presidents work along in the government with little help from Congress, administration officials, or other advisers.* In the foreign policy speeches, ambassadors, cabinet secretaries, or joint chiefs are rarely mentioned. The same holds for economic speeches where congressional committees, the Council of Economic Advisers, the Federal Reserve, and other decision makers are curiously absent. In the major addresses all references to Congress (including to a leader, a committee, or Congress itself) form about 4 percent of the references to any American actors. Executive branch references (to an individual, a department, or general reference to advisers) form about 3 percent. In contrast, "presidential references," to be explained below, form about 80 percent. This dominance holds for all presidents and is seen also in the minor addresses.

It is interesting that Congress appears active only in planning or returning from its adjournment. It does not oppose the president—it merely goes home. "Congress has gone home," presidents tell the nation. A vital part of the nation's business must wait until Congress returns. This holds for presidents of the same or opposing party as the party in control of Congress; and it holds for those, like Johnson and Ford, who had previously spent long years as congressional leaders. The ex-minority leader Ford is as eager as any president to paint a picture of the vacationing, dallying Congress, never in Washington when the serious work must be done. The exceptional cases when presidents admit facing opposition from Congress stand out by their very infrequency: Truman (an ex-Senator) twice; Ford (a House leader) once; and Reagan (with no experience in Congress) twice.

For a second part of the picture, *the work of American government is carried on primarily by the President, the American people, and the nation.* These are the same thing and may be used interchangeably with each other. The president equals the nation and equals the American people. Together, these three dominate the activity that is presented, forming about 80 percent of the references to the American participants. While foreign policy speeches do show other nations and governments at work, the president remains the only American featured.

These three are used interchangeably, as shown by the use of the plural pronoun "we." This is not merely the "royal we," employed when a reference to "I" would be too awkward or personal. The word is used in several senses, often within the same argument and the same sentence. One finds a pattern of usage independent of individual style. So Reagan says, we (the administration) propose to eliminate the Energy Department because we (the American people) do not need an energy program. Kennedy says, we (the administration) need an education bill because we are going to have all these children . . .

One can see this presidential dominance in a number of ways: by a content analysis; by a more detailed critical analysis of the text; by looking at all references (nouns and pronouns); or by looking only at the subjects of the sentences, *that is,* the main actors of the speeches. For example, if one looks at all references in the major addresses to any American actor, whether an individual or an institution, one finds that

> 63 percent are to We, the Nation, or the American people
> (or synonym)
> 20 percent are to I, the President, this Administration
> (or synonym)
> 17 percent are to all other American references.

These 17 percent include all references to Congress, to executive branch agencies and personnel, general references to advisers, all mention of groups in the country (business, farmers, and labor, wage earners and the unemployed), American soldiers past and present, historical figures, and all others. In comparison with all these people, the presidential references total more than 80 percent.

This finding holds for the major and minor speeches and for the different audiences addressed. The particular kind of address will determine which of these other references are mentioned more—soldiers in the foreign policy speeches, groups to the groups themselves. As one might expect, the informal "I" is more commonly heard in the minor remarks, almost equalling the "We the nation" references. There are ways that presidents adapt speeches to an audience, but the basic self-presentation is not adapted. They are the single major actor in the government and the synonym for the nation.

Most importantly, this picture of government holds across presidencies, from the 1940s to the 1980s. When one looks at sentence subjects, no substantial differences are found for party, time period, or electoral status in the frequency with which presidents cite all other actors, whether American or not, or identify themselves with the nation. Democrats mention other actors 31 percent of the time and Republicans 26 percent. Truman, Johnson, and Ford, who came to the White House through succession, are no more likely to cite other actors than the other presidents are. In other words, they are as willing as the other presidents to present themselves along with the nation and the American people as the only major actor in the government. The same holds for what can be called the postimperial presidents: Ford, Carter, and Reagan. They refer to all other actors 26 percent of the time, while their five predecessors cited other actors 28 percent of the time. They are no less imperial than the earlier presidents in asserting a dominant role in government.

So, in his economic address in June 1981, Reagan asks the American people to support his tax-reform proposal: "In these six months, we've done so much and have come so far. It's been the power of millions of people like you who have determined that we will make American great again. You have made the difference up to now. You will make the difference again. Let us not stop now." The pronouns shift from the first to the second person and back: the president is simultaneously one of the American people and a leader of the people asking for their support. Tax reform is not a matter for White House advisers, economists, or compromises between House and Senate committees. It will be created by the president and the American people, both "we" and "you."

In terms of the introductory discussion, the same picture of government is carried on across the years. It is not a government of pluralism and a separation of powers, but a unitary system where the leader can speak for the nation and the people. This, at least, is what the presidents say the office and the government are like.

For a third part of the picture, *presidents are unique and without peers: there is only one president.* Ford makes an exception in his remarks on taking office and speaks of Nixon and the Nixon family. Reagan discusses past economic policy (much more in fact than others discussed the past). But beyond these cases, presidents give little sense that others have stood in the same place, said the same things, and faced the same problems before. Less than one in fifteen of the major addresses mentions any past administration even once. These tend to be the administrations of Washington, Lincoln, Jefferson, and FDR. Almost none mentions the immediate past. Truman mentions Roosevelt once and Johnson refers once to the Kennedy assassination. Reagan speaks of "building on the Camp

David accords," but does not explain that they were Carter's accords and not his own.

Some differences are observable among the presidents, as seen in table 5.1. Republicans Reagan and Ford are more willing than their Democratic counterparts to mention presidents of the past, including the Democratic Franklin Roosevelt. Since Republican presidents usually need more bipartisan support in Congress than the Democrats do, the references to FDR may be a calculated ones. Reagan's references to Truman all occurred in a 1983 speech calling for bipartisan support for Nicaraguan aid. Since Truman needed GOP help to get his foreign aid programs passed, Reagan is calling on the Democrats to return the favor.

The differences, of course, are small in relation to the overall consistent pattern. The recent past is erased along with the recent presidents. Everything starts anew. So, each president says "We will now go forward. . . ," "We will now begin." It is amusing in fact to see the same words repeated —that this time we will really begin.

TABLE 5.1

References to Past Presidents: Inaugural, Foreign Policy, and Economic Policy Speeches[a]

President Speaking	Number of References President Referred to		
	Four Great Presidents[b]	Immediate Predecessor	All Other Twentieth-Century Presidents
Truman	2	(2)[c]	0
Eisenhower	4	0	0
Kennedy	0	0	0
Johnson	0	1	0
Nixon	1	0	0
Ford	4	3	0
Carter	0	0	0
Reagan	9	2	4
Total	20	8	4
Total Pages = 155			

Notes: [a]All references are counted when the president is referred to by name. The sentence is the unit of analysis, with the exception that multisentence quotations are counted only once.
[b]Washington, Jefferson, Lincoln, Franklin Roosevelt.
[c]Since Truman's immediate predecessor is Franklin Roosevelt, the references are included in both columns of the table.
Source: Barbara Hinckley, *The Symbolic Presidency* (Chatham, N.J.: Chatham House, 1988).

Truman says	We will advance
Kennedy	Let us now begin
Johnson	Let us seek to go forward
Nixon	Let us go forward
Ford	We must go forward now
Reagan	Let us begin.

This theme of a new beginning is central to the American myth, as many writers point out, and is not limited to presidents. America is the New World. The American Revolution, as James Robertson explains, created a new nation and erased the past: hence, we celebrate this charter myth by a continual process of creation and erasing.[10] But it is said that when people cannot learn from the mistakes of the past, they are doomed to repeat them. In this case, there is no past and no predecessors. The past is symbolically abolished with each new administration, and, with the same words repeated, everything starts again.

Some variation occurs in the presentations from one president to another. The nonelected Ford relies more on the first-person "I" than other presidents do in his remarks on taking office. (In fact, Ford chose not to call his first speech on taking office in August 1974, an inaugural address.) Reagan is more willing than the other presidents to talk of negotiations with Congress. Kennedy is the most likely to mention foreign nations and Johnson to refer to domestic groups. While the minor addresses convey a similar picture of government, they show differences in the groups that are addressed. Truman talks to Masonic groups and Nixon to football teams; Kennedy likes gatherings with foreign diplomats in the White House. Johnson and Carter add visits with blacks and women's groups to their schedules, while their Republican successors in office do not. Ford speaks to party groups more frequently than the other presidents do. Against these differences, the similarities in presentation are all the more striking, holding across parties, diverse circumstances, and very different personal styles.

In short, one finds an *institutionalized* portrayal of the office carried on by the presidents themselves. Circumstances change, advisers rise and fall from favor, speech writers come and go, but the same picture is presented and carried on across time. Paradoxically, this institution features an individual and a new beginning—it denies its "institutional" character. Nevertheless, it carries on the same emphasis and the same denial from one presidency to the next. In short, an important expectation of this institution is that it is autonomous from past administrations and from the rest of the business of government. New policies and new approaches will be developed by new presidents. That is the expectation—and the promise—of presidential leadership, repeated with each new incumbent who comes to office.

OTHER EXPECTATIONS

Presidents are not alone of course in the way they present their office. Writers speak of a "cult of the presidency" carried on by academics, journalists, and others, whereby the president is cast as the single powerful head of the government and sole representative of the nation.[11] Journalists have been criticized for summarizing an entire administration's work as "the president's program" or translating a complex news event into a White House story. Look at elementary school weekly readers and see the current incumbent placed along with Washington and Lincoln. Or think of the famous picture of Kennedy alone at the Oval Office window. Socialization studies trace the cognitive process by which presidents become the symbol of the nation: other institutions are learned about in relation to them.[12] So, Congress becomes a group that "helps the president."

The public too wipes out the past and gives support to the new incumbent no matter what the past incumbent has done. Ford's approval rating on his inauguration day was as high as Nixon's was when he first came to office. Nothing in the interim had changed that general support. In a clever study published after Watergate, a national sample was asked if the Watergate crisis had "weakened their confidence in the presidency as an institution." A large majority said yes. But then the sample was asked all the standard support questions that had been asked before (Would you support the president in time of crisis, and so forth) and the same high percentages answered as they had always done.[13] No sign of that shaken confidence appeared. In these cases, the public is doing what the presidents do—wiping out the past and reasserting its support for the office.

This is not to say that all textbook writers or journalists follow the cult; many in fact have been sharply critical of it. Recent academic writing points out how little presidents are able to do.[14] Majorities of the public can disapprove of a policy the president argues strongly for—and majorities can disapprove of the way he is doing his job. Nevertheless, it is important to see the convergence in expectations as well as the discrepancies. *The presidents themselves are carrying on the cult* and may be its most vigorous supporters.

Even the criticisms by the press and public can be taken as signs of the strength of the expectations: presidents are criticized or lampooned for not being as powerful or blameless as they are supposed to be. So, the more individuals in the Reagan and Nixon administrations are blamed for the scandals of their time, the less the office is touched. Many thousand pages of testimony, final reports, and press summaries document exactly what Oliver North and John Poindexter did, what Bill Casey said and when he said it. In the amount of pages of print available to the public, the Iran-Contra autopsies must be second only to the Watergate writing. But all this detail helps keep the individuals separate from the office. People psychoanalyze Nixon, joke about Reagan's attention span, and typecast North as a wild man or cult hero. But this ton of writing does more than "explain" an event—it locates, or buries, it in individual trivia. The particular circumstances, in all their idiosyncratic detail, will not be reproduced: hence confidence is shaken in one president but not in the presidency—and the slate can be wiped clean on the next Inauguration Day.

Presidents, journalists and academics, the public—all help to shape the expectations of the office. There is no one single agent or simple causal explanation. Rather, institutions are formed from the shared expectations of many people, reinforcing each other over time. Presidents shape the office, but they respond as well to the expectations of others. They are successful in fact, in winning election or governing in the White House, insofar as they best embody what these expectations might be. "I tell you that which you yourselves do know," said Mark Antony to the Roman citizens on the death of Caesar.[15] Antony, the expert in public opinion, knew that the most effective leaders say what the public wants to be true. Modern presidents follow that ancient principle and so help define future public expectations.

The presidency was left open, under the Constitution, to grow and change with the developing nation. It could adapt to historical circumstances and become what people wanted it to be. But this means that those who describe the office, and so shape the expectations of others, need to think about what they are doing. Presidents since Wilson began to say that they were a world leader, and the public came to accept that role. Congress passed legislation to help meet these expectations, creating among other things a National Security Council and a CIA. What people now say the president is becomes in a very real sense the building blocks for the future. All institutions are shaped by the expectations of people. But because of the constitutional openness, the presidency is particularly subject to this shaping. Therefore,the expectations we see carried on by the presidents themselves have importance for the future of the office and for discussions about what that future should be.

IMPLICATIONS FOR REFORM

In times of scandal or disarray at the White House, various reforms are called for. The president is too strong, or the president is too weak, or the president needs help, or the president needs *something,* to cure whatever is wrong at the time. But *some of the problems may not actually exist*—they may be artifacts of the unrealistic expectations. If presidents are expected to produce economic prosperity and solve all social problems, then the failure to do so suggests something is wrong. But since they cannot do these things and no reforms will make them able to, the office may be functioning as well as possible.

Contrary to the pictures of government the presidents present, one can state some obvious facts. First, the government is not unitary, headed by a single powerful individual. In fact, the American president is much more limited under the Constitution than most other heads of state. Second, the president is only one human being with limits on time and attention. Most of the decisions of government will be made by others and never reach the president at all. Third, problems of government continue over time. Some are rooted in the conflicts of international and domestic politics; some are unsolvable. Policies, too, continue over time, with incremental changes on a base of past decisions. Presidents serve no more than eight years, while bureaucrats and the average member of Congress stay in office much longer. In short, the government does not start anew on Inauguration Day. Most of its problems and its personnel continue.

Presidents know these realities of course and much of the public does too. But to bring the dissonant reality into line with the expectations, one is committed to call for reforms. It is a way of admitting the reality while keeping alive the expectations. Since the emperor must be wearing clothes, something else must be wrong with the parade.

Some of the problems may be caused by the unrealistic expectations. During the Watergate hearings, one White House witness after another justified wrongdoing on the ground that helping the president was the most important thing that could be done for the country at the time. One such witness was the former attorney general, the chief law enforcement officer, John Mitchell. If the president is a synonym for the nation, and what is good for the president becomes what is good for the nation, that kind of justification follows. Against the constitutional principle of "a government of laws and not of men," presidents present a government of men and not of laws.

During the Iran-Contra hearings, several witnesses blamed Congress for the illegal actions carried on in the White House. If Congress had not interfered with the president's role as foreign policymaker, then such extreme measures would not have been necessary. This sounds analogous to the car thief blaming the owner for leaving the keys in the ignition, but it follows from the picture of government we have previously seen. If Congress is seen as a rather trivial participant in government—even when it is not on vacation—that kind of argument makes sense. Against the principle of checks and balances, presidents present a government in which only one individual makes policy for the nation. A congressional law becomes interference with that role.

The problem is that presidents may come to believe in their own images. Writing before Watergate, George Reedy warned of an atmosphere in the White House leading presidents to think they were free of the rules governing ordinary mortals. Unique and virtually alone, with only the ghosts of Washington and Lincoln for company, they would begin to believe in their own exaltation.[16] The symbol would become the reality. Isolated from ordinary political realities, they could believe that what was good for the president was good for the nation and that Congress should stop meddling in serious affairs of state.

This atmosphere extends to the advisers too, who can bask in the reflected glory. "The President," says Reedy, "is treated with all the reverence due a monarch. No one ever invites him to go soak his head."[17] But no one wants to tell the nation to go soak its head. And if the White House must engage in the kind of thinking that carries on two contradictory realities, this can impair judgment even further. By this argument, changing the structure of White House advising will not change the quality of its decisions. One would need to change the perceptions of the presidents and their advisers.

Many writers point out the disturbing tendency of symbolism over substance in government. They see presidents encouraged to lie, fake, and mislead others, and so preoccupied with symbol manipulation and information control that they do not have time for other activities. But it should not be surprising that candidates are packaged in election campaigns, or that once in office they present themselves in misleading ways. Candidates are selected who can best perform the duties of the office and the duties are to make these idealized projections. Hence, if people would like an office of more substance and less appearance, reforms would have to come from changing expectations.

Can presidents lie and present misleading information to the American people? Why, they are encouraged to do so in every public presentation they make. And why should they need to do so? Because the job they are expected to do is so at odds with the job they can actually do. So, again, if people want fewer cover-ups, secret arms deals, and other dishonesties in the White House, they might ask for a more fundamental honesty in presentations of the office.

Finally, *the expectations may obscure problems that do exist.* Reforms cannot be made if they are not identified. The past, and the mistakes of the past, are abolished with each new administration: the lessons of the Old World cannot help the new. So, do presidents come to the office of Washington and Lincoln, or of Grant, Harding, and Nixon too? If scandals and abuses of power could occur in the past, why should we be surprised when they occur in the present? No changes have been made in the past ten years that suggest they could not occur. Or occur again in another ten years.

Watergate was seen as a problem of Nixon and his advisers, the fault traced to the individual in office at the time. The Iran affair, too, was seen as a problem with people who assumed too much power and a president who was not in control. Ten years from now there will be other special circumstances to explain the next set of revelations. This does not absolve the individuals from blame. But it suggests the individual in office is not a sufficient explanation. Just like the presidents, we abolish the past and the mistakes of the past. We put Watergate behind us. We will put Irangate behind us. And the next president will enter the office of Washington and Lincoln and say, "Let us begin."

BEYOND REFORM

What might result from challenging the three expectations that presidents so consistently present? If presidents are not alone in the government, what should be known about the selection and job assignment of advisers? Should people be told before the election who will make decisions in the President's name? What should be asked by way of regular consultation with Congress on key foreign policy questions and what demands made on Congress for oversight that would continue beyond occasions making the front-page news? If presidents are not expected to perform impossible missions, there might be less pressure to evade normal political channels —to use covert action and misuse national security claims.

If presidents are not synonyms for the nation, might the burden of ceremonial duties be lessened, even if marginally—all the appearances and two-minute talks in the Rose Garden that now fill each president's day? Obviously these are political acts, designed to bolster public support. But it has been estimated that the trips alone and other appearances outside the White House fill about one-third of a president's time in office.[18] Should some of this time be spent on other activities? If the ceremonial skills were even marginally less important, would different kinds of candidates be selected? Would different advisers, with other background experience, be sought?

If presidents are not unique, but hold their positions for a short point in time in a long run of government, what should be asked by way of presidential "leadership" and "success"? If missions were defined more realistically, might presidents be judged with more accuracy and held more accountable for what they might actually be able to do? And could we then afford to call on the experience of *past* presidents, now forced to maintain an awkward retirement with only the occasional honorary degree or conference with foreign dignitaries to occupy their time. No one, it is said, can prepare for the presidency. But these individuals have prepared—and have the results of their experience to offer. Writers point out a paradox of experience and influence. Presidents lose support the longer they are in office: hence those least experienced in making White House decisions are the most likely to succeed.[19] When everything is made new it is also made inexperienced. If the past could be acknowledged, even if only marginally, it might be used to improve the quality of government.

These questions point to a more fundamental one—of what people want the office to be. It is surprising that it has not been asked, given all the attention paid to public opinion polls. People watch carefully the ups and downs of the president's "job approval" rating, even though they are not sure what the question means or what kind of answers it elicits. Studies tell us that the presidents watch them too and style their behavior accordingly. So, political scientists might devise ways to ask about the range of expectations held for the office. Do people want a separation of powers or a unitary system of government? Do they believe in a new beginning every four or eight years and one individual in control of the government? If the president's job were defined more realistically, would support for the office rise or fall? Are the current ways of presenting the office necessary for legitimacy or do they create more cynicism and disillusionment instead? These can be cast as empirical questions. If the office is shaped—and changed—by expectations, we need to look more closely at what these expectations might be.

NOTES

1. Alexander George, *Presidential Decision-Making in Foreign Policy* (Boulder, Colo.: Westview, 1980); Irving Janis, *Groupthink*, 2d ed. (Boston: Houghton Mifflin, 1982).

2. See Michael Grossman and Martha Kumar, *Portraying the President* (Baltimore: Johns Hopkins University Press, 1980), pp. 263, 264.

3. In a very large literature, see for example, George Edwards, *The Public Presidency* (New York: St. Martin's Press, 1983); John Mueller, "Presidential Popularity from Truman to Johnson," *American Political Science Review*, March 1970, 18–24; Samuel Kernell, "Explaining Presidential Popularity," *American Political Science Review*, June 1978, 506–22; James Bond and Richard Fleisher, "The Limits of Presidential Popularity as a Source of Influence in the U.S. House," *Legislative Studies Quarterly*, February 1980, 69–78.

4. Paul Light, *The President's Agenda* (Baltimore: Johns Hopkins University Press, 1982); Samuel Kernell, *Going Public* (Washington, D.C.: Congressional Quarterly Press, 1986); Lyn Ragsdale, "The Politics of Presidential Speechmaking," *American Political Science Review*, December 1984, 971–84; Joseph Pika, "Interest Groups and the White House: Comparing Administrations," unpublished paper, Political Science Department, University of Delaware.

5. Charles Ostrom and Brian Job, "The President and the Political Use of Force," *American Political Science Review*, June 1986, 541–66.

120 *Barbara Hinckley*

6. Philip Selznik, *Leadership in Administration* (New York: Harper and Row, 1957), see esp. pp. 38–40.

7. *The Public Papers of the Presidents of the United States* (Washington, D.C.: Government Printing Office). The *Public Papers* are available in annual volumes from George Washington to the present.

8. Selecting the first three years allows comparability across presidents and excludes any election-year effects. The years are drawn as follows: Truman, 1949–1951; Eisenhower, 1953–1955; Kennedy, 1961–1963; Johnson, 1965–1967; Nixon, 1969–1971; Ford, 1974–1975; Carter, 1977–1979; Reagan, 1981–1983.

9. Barbara Hinckley, *The Symbolic Presidency* (Chatham, N.J.: Chatham House, 1988); see esp. chapter 2. Other studies showing the similarity of presidential statements over time include Ragsdale, cited above; Roderick Hart, *The Sound of Leadership* (Chicago: University of Chicago Press, 1987); Theodore Windt, *Presidential Rhetoric (1961 to the Present)*, 3d ed. (Dubuque, Iowa: Kendall-Hunt, 1983); and Dante Germino, *The Inaugural Addresses of American Presidents* (Lanham, Md.: University Press of America, 1984).

10. James Robertson, *American Myth, American Reality* (New YorK: Hill and Wang, 1980).

11. See Thomas Cronin, *The State of the Presidency*, 2d ed. (Boston: Little, Brown, 1980), pp. 75–116.

12. See Fred Greenstein, "What the President Means to Americans," in James David Barber, ed., *Choosing the President* (New York: American Assembly, 1974), pp. 121–48. For discussion of these studies, see Hinckley, *Problems of the Presidency* (Glenview, Ill.: Scott, Foresman, 1985), chapter 2.

13. Jack Dennis, "Dimensions of Public Support for the Presidency," Midwest Political Science Association paper, May 1975, see esp. tables 2 and 3. The tables are reprinted in Hinckley, *Problems of the Presidency*, p. 26.

14. See Hugh Heclo and Lester Salamon, *The Illusion of Presidential Government* (Boulder, Colo.: Westview, 1981); Godfrey Hodgson, *All Things to All Men* (New York: Simon & Schuster, 1980).

15. William Shakespeare, *Julius Ceasar*, act 3, sc. 2, line 228.

16. George Reedy, *The Twilight of the Presidency* (New York: World, 1980). A revised edition has been published in 1987.

17. Ibid., p. 18.

18. Samuel Kernell, "The Presidency and the People," in Michael Nelson, ed., *The Presidency and the Political System* (Washington, D.C.: Congressional Quarterly Press, 1984), p. 243.

19. See Light, *The President's Agenda*.

SIX

Presidents, the Economy, and Elections: A Principal-Agent Perspective

Nathaniel Beck

Why did American economic policymakers induce a steep recession in 1981–1982? Why did those policymakers, including President Reagan, feel that it was so necessary to vigorously fight inflation? There are many answers to these questions, but one line of inquiry is to argue that presidents want to be reelected, and so they must make policy in accord with what the voters desire. There is a long tradition in political science of looking at the linkages between mass politics and elite behavior. The linkage is obviously based on elections, but the exact nature of this linkage is perhaps more complicated than might appear at first glance. In this essay I shall look at how presidents make domestic economic policy, using the perspective of this linkage. But first it is necessary to flesh out the nature of the linkage. I do so using the metaphor of the electorate and the president as being in a "principal and agent" relationship. After an ab-

This chapter is based on papers presented at the European Consortium for Political Research, Joint Meetings, held in April 1987 in Amsterdam at a conference on Elections and the Economy in the United States and Western Europe held in May 1987 in Bellagio, Italy, and at the Political Economy Workshop, Duke University, in January 1988. I would like to thank the conference participants for their comments. In particular, I would like to thank Chip Chappell and Bill Keech for their helpful comments as well as their pioneering work in this area.

stract consideration of that metaphor, I use it to see if we can better understand American economic policy over the past thirty-five years.

THE METAPHOR OF PRINCIPAL AND AGENT

Imagine a fairly large group of people getting together to undertake a wide variety of tasks. Assume that the tasks involve the provision of public goods so that market or other types of decentralized mechanisms would not be ideal. In other words, assume that some form of centralized authority or decisionmaking is necessary for the performance of these social tasks. Also assume that the variety and complexity of the tasks makes it difficult if not impossible to enumerate the tasks requiring performance at any given moment.

There are many ways such a group could attempt to organize, but one obvious way would be to choose a leader to undertake (or at least oversee) the various tasks. Such a leader would need a wide grant of authority, given the variety and complexity of the tasks he or she must perform. The problem is then to keep the leader from abusing his or her grant of authority.

One solution would be to narrow the scope of the grant. But this might raise the cost of making new grants as new tasks arose, or as the nature of the tasks changed. A narrow grant of authority severely limited the American government under the Articles of Confederation. Dissatisfaction with this narrow grant led to the new Constitution, which gave the president a wide grant of executive power.

Another solution would be to impose some fundamental limitations on the leader, that is, to write a set of rules guaranteeing that the leader could not infringe on various protected rights. These fundamental rules would still give the leader wide latitude as long as he or she did not stray outside a wide path of acceptable behavior. The American Constitution contains many such limits on political leaders, although our leaders have wide authority as long as they stay within those limits.

A third solution proposed by the authors of the *Federalist Papers* was to make a split grant of authority and then "pit ambition against ambition." Congress would keep the president from abusing his grant, and the president would behave similarly toward the Congress. A system of multiple leaders may be less efficient, but it does make it more difficult for any leader to abuse the grant of authority.

The authors of the *Federalist* envisaged a republican form of government. Popular elections would thus be a mechanism by which leaders could be controlled by the citizenry. In principle the republican mechanism could take several forms. Different individuals could run for leader, with a variety of possible vote-counting rules for choice of leader. Elections for leader could be held periodically, with or without the possibility of leaders being allowed to succeed themselves. Alternatively, a confirmation election on the current leader could be held at regularly scheduled intervals, with some choice mechanism necessary for selecting a new leader if the current leader were rejected. These elections need not be regularly scheduled, but might instead be recall elections, taking place whenever a large enough portion of the group appears dissatisfied with current leadership.

In the United States we use all of these types of electoral mechanisms to control our leaders. Presidential elections, which are the focus of this essay, are contested by two or more individuals (or parties) at regularly scheduled intervals. Every four years the populace is asked whether they wish the president (or at least his party) to continue in office, or whether his opponent should occupy the White House.[1] The United States does not use a confirmation election to decide whether the president should be allowed to stay in office, but many political analysts view American elections as looking very much like such an election. Many Americans seem to vote "retrospectively," that is, instead of comparing the two candidates they decide whether to vote for or against the incumbent on the basis of his performance during the previous term.[2] American presidential elections thus look much like a referendum, where voters vote yes or no, but with the vote concerning whether to keep the incumbent (or his party) in office rather than the enactment of some policy. (I use the terms referendum voting and retrospective voting interchangeably in this essay.)

If leaders wish to stay in office, then upcoming elections should cause leaders to respond in some manner to the demands of the group. Since on most issues the group will not speak clearly, and since there will be many more issues or tasks than referenda or votes, the electoral mechanism will still allow leaders wide latitude. But leaders who abuse their grant of authority can be punished. Only leaders who are content to be deposed can ignore the demands of the citizenry in a democracy.

The relationship between the leader and the group is one of agent and principal. A principal wishes to have some task performed, but for some reason cannot do so itself. The principal therefore must choose an agent to perform the task or tasks, and the question is how the principal can get its agent to act in the interest of the principal. The problem becomes critical when, as so often happens, it is difficult or costly for the principal to monitor the activities of its agent, and the preferences of the principal and agent do not coincide. Agents not acting in their principal's interest are said to "shirk."

"The new economics of organization" has found the concept of principal-agent relationships to be of great value.[3] A good example is how an individual manages his or her investments. Most of us lack the skill to do this ourselves, so we hire an agent, an investment firm. The problem is that we wish our agent to maximize our income, but our agent, the investment firm, wishes to maximize its own income. How can we get our investment firm to behave diligently, that is, to manage our money wisely? How can we keep the firm from shirking, that is, increasing its own income at our expense (churning) or failing to undertake costly activities, such as research, on our behalf?

If we could monitor the firm's behavior, then we could force the firm to act in our interest (or move our business elsewhere). But monitoring the firm is at least as difficult and costly as managing our own investments. We can observe the profits our investment firm generates for us, but unfortunately there is no straightforward relationship between the activities of the firm and the results it generates. In bull markets any investment firm can generate good results, and in bear markets even the most diligent firm may lose money for us. Is there some type of contract that we can write to make our firm behave more diligently? In general the answer is yes, and the trick is to make the firm's profits depend on our profits.

The situation is much more difficult in the political arena. Here the principal is the electorate and the agent is the elected leader (whom I shall call the president). There is no longer a single principal; the principal is a collectivity. The electorate needs an agent because of the difficulty of collective action. What is shirking in the electoral context? Political leaders hardly seem lazy. Sometimes they steal, but hopefully this is the exceptional situation. Shirking, in the electoral context, consists of leaders carrying out the policies they want rather than doing what the electorate wants.

In the principal-agent perspective elected leaders should behave, in Edmund Burke's famous categorization, as a delegate rather than a trustee. The issue then becomes how to make the leader be such a delegate. This is hardly a noncontroversial assumption. Remember that Burke himself argued, in a parliamentary context, that elected leaders should behave as trustees and not delegates. In the principal-agent context it is impossible for voters to trust the leader's pledge to be a good "trustee." Leaders can exploit their superior information if voters merely expect them to behave as trustees. The critical factor for understanding presidential behavior is the existence of future elections, for it is those elections which keep the president "honest," that is, force him or her to worry about the demands of the populace.

In this essay I shall use the principal-agent metaphor to examine the role of presidential elections in the making of policy. In particular I look at how the modern American electorate can and does (and doesn't) control the president in the arena of economic policy. Economic policy is of interest in and of itself, but it is also an arena where shirking is possible. Presidents come to office with their own economic priorities, which may not be the priorities of the electorate. The electorate can observe the outcomes of the president's economic policy, but it cannot observe the making of that policy.

This inability to observe policy-making makes it possible for the president to try to fool the populace by creating a temporary election day boom (a "political business cycle"). Political economists have devoted much effort to the study of the political business cycle. The principal-agent approach should be able to throw new light on this question. Before dealing with that question, however, I must first discuss how the electorate might go about controlling the president. This discussion will remain at the metaphorical level.

ELECTORAL CONTROL OF THE PRESIDENT METAPHOR

The typical question in principal-agent models is how to design a set of incentives for the agent so that he or she will not shirk. In the electoral context this would be translated into the question "what form of voter behavior would best make for responsive leaders?" This question, unfortunately, is very difficult to answer. Scholars know very little about principal-agent problems with more than one principal, and the electorate contains a vast number of principals. The only proposed solutions so far involves the various principals selling their rights to an intermediary and this solution is inappropriate in the electoral context.

In an ingenious article, Ferejohn (1986) has attempted a partial solution by assuming a homogeneous electorate. This assumption eliminates the problem of multiple principals. He also takes liberties with the political definition of shirking. Presidents viewed as agents shirk when they do not do what the populace, in some sense, wants. But if the president is not doing what the people want, it is difficult to figure out what the president will do. To get around this problem Ferejohn assumes that the executive produces some outcome that the voters value. For our purposes we can take this outcome as the state of the economy. To produce desirable outcomes the president must use effort, and Ferejohn assumes that such effort is costly. Ferejohn therefore assumes that voters desire a lot of presidential effort while presidents desire to give less effort.

The situation becomes interesting as a principal-agent problem when the electorate cannot directly monitor presidential effort. All the electorate can do is to monitor economic outcomes. This would present no problem if there were a simple relationship between effort and outcomes, but that relationship is only probabilistic. To put it loosely, luck and effort come together to generate outcomes, and a lazy executive could be lucky while a hardworking one could be unlucky.

Ferejohn then assumes that leaders want to stay in office. Leaders are chosen in an election, but candidates' promises are thought to be irrelevant. In the Ferejohn model all candidates would always promise maximal effort, but then would always try to renege.[4] Thus elections must be referenda, in which the leader will be allowed to continue in office if he or she did a good enough job. If the electorate wants good outcomes, how should it decide whether to return the incumbent to office?

While Ferejohn's work is very abstract, it does look something like what we think of as presidential politics. Some presidents seem to command a lot of respect for their economic policy but, for reasons not under their control (luck) they are associated with a bad economy. Herbert Hoover may have been a prototypically unlucky president in terms of the economy; most economic historians do not blame him for the Great Depression, and, by many accounts (for example, Stein 1984) he followed fairly reasonable policies. Yet the voters chose not to continue the Republicans in office.

Jimmy Carter also seems to have had bad economic luck. He may not have been responsible for increases in the price of oil or the sharp downturn in the economy in 1980, but in November 1980 the voters decided to back another horse. His successor has generally not received high marks for his economic policies. But, whether because of moderating oil prices or good harvests or whatever, the voters decided that economic outcomes had been good enough to continue Ronald Reagan in office in 1984.

Given the difficulty of observing a president's economic policies it seems sensible for voters to look at the outcomes produced by the president. We could argue for years about whether Carter's policies were correct, but it does not take nearly so long to assess economic outcomes during his administration.[5] The situation is similar, with a different outcome, for the Reagan administration. Were oil prices low under Reagan because of Carter's conservation policy or Reagan's foreign policy? Were oil prices high under Carter because of Carter's incompetence or mistakes made by Henry Kissinger in 1973? We could argue about those questions for days, but oil prices clearly rose rapidly under Carter and fell under Reagan.

The problem with observing outcomes is that presidents who are lucky will then have an incentive to shirk. The problem for the electorate is to define a voting rule that minimizes this shirking. Ferejohn's basic insight is that if voters demand too much of the president, that is, if they only vote for reelection if outcomes were excellent, then presidents who cannot provide excellent outcomes because of bad luck have no incentive to produce desirable outcomes. On the other hand, if the threshold for reelection is too low, presidents can again get away with shirking. Thus the threshold must be set somewhere in the middle.

Ferejohn also shows that if the electorate is diverse, voters do better if they vote on the basis of societal outcomes rather than their own particular outcomes. This is because if voters vote on the basis of their own outcomes the president can always promise to reward 51 percent of the electorate with the other 49 percent doing very poorly. These other voters would then have an incentive to offer to support the incumbent if they only received minimally better outcomes, but then the losing 49 percent would have an incentive to make the same offer, and so forth. In the end, an electorate that voted on the basis of private outcomes would allow the president to shirk a lot.

Ferejohn's argument is that the electorate should agree to bind itself to vote on the basis of social rather than private outcomes. This eliminates the possibility of the president making offers to 51 percent of the electorate. Thus voters should look at the overall unemployment rate and not whether they themselves were unemployed. If the electorate voted on the latter basis then presidents would have no incentive to reduce unemployment for a permanent class of the unemployed. If, for example, 10 percent of the populace were permanently unemployed but everyone else was doing moderately well, the president could expect reelection despite the horrible economic circumstances if voters voted on the basis of their own well-being.[6]

Researchers have found that the American electorate does seem to vote on the basis of overall societal outcomes and not on the basis of how well the individual voter has done.[7] This type of voting has been called "sociotropic." The original researchers contrasted sociotropic with self-interested voting, but Ferejohn has shown that sociotropic voting can be self-interested.

Ferejohn's incredibly oversimplified model yields some interesting results about elections. But it is his basic way of looking at elections that is even more useful. His approach stresses the costs of the principal's monitoring of the agent's behavior. The electorate cannot observe what its leaders do, only what they produce. There is no simple relationship between what leaders do and what outcomes are produced. Better policy may, on average, produce better outcomes, but some leaders are lucky and some are not. There may be inflation because leaders are doing a bad job, or there may be inflation because of bad harvests. Ferejohn stresses the unimportance of promises about what the leader will do in the future. In the principal-agent perspective on elections, candidates always have the incentive to promise a lot and produce very little. It is only the challenge of being reelected that causes presidents to do what the populace wants.

MONITORING COSTS, ECONOMIC POLICY, AND POLITICAL BUSINESS CYCLES

What does the principal-agent approach tell us about presidential economic policy-making? Voters can easily observe some economic outcomes such as their own financial well-being; with more difficulty they can observe some simple indicators of the state of the economy, such as the unemployment rate (available on the nightly TV news or in the daily newspaper). They could, at higher cost, observe more complicated but presumably better indicators such as the growth rate of real per capita personal income. At even greater cost they could observe predictions about the future economy; such predictions may or may not be reliable. The electorate cannot directly observe economic policy-making, although at high cost it could observe some indicators of policy, such as whether unemployment is above or below its natural rate, the size of the deficit, or the growth rate of the money supply. What should the electorate do under such circumstances?

Obviously the answer depends on monitoring costs and the importance of voting to the citizenry. It is typically assumed that voters would not find it in their interest to obtain much costly information since their vote is only one among millions.[8] If, on the other hand, voters use only the most easily available economic information, they may make incorrect decisions. For example, if voters monitor inflation, then they may reward presidents who are lucky. Presidents can hardly ensure the good weather necessary for bountiful harvests, but they may reap the rewards of good weather if voters look at outcomes rather than policy. The principal-agent perspective sees the possibility of leaders taking advantage of good luck, but regards that possibility as an unfortunate consequence of costly information.

If voters evaluate presidents on the basis of easily observable measures of the economy, then presidents may have an incentive to engage in strategic behavior which is not in the electorate's interest. It is possible for presidents to create "political business cycles" if voters evaluate the incumbent on the basis of current and past economic outcomes. Presidents can create a political business cycle by pumping up the economy right before election day to create an electoral boom. Such a boom may be only temporary, and may have bad long-term consequences for inflation. (The basic economic theory is that the pumping up first causes unemployment to fall. Inflation eventually rises, but only after some time. In the long run all we have is higher inflation, with no lower unemployment, but at election time the voter observes lower unemployment with little extra inflation.) But, if voters look only at past and current outcomes, these bad consequences will not enter their electoral decision.

The president can be even more devious if voters have short memories. In this case the president can induce a recession early in his term so as to lower inflationary expectations. This will delay the onset of the extra inflation caused by the electoral boom, and hence will allow the president to run a bigger electoral boom without suffering the electoral costs of high inflation. But this depends critically on voters forgetting the early term costs of the recession. From a monitoring perspective it clearly is more plausible that voters ignore the postelection consequences of the electoral manipulation than that they forget the past bad times; the post

election consequences can only be predicted theoretically whereas the
early term recession is quite easy to monitor (and remember). If voters
only observe outcomes and ignore policy and forecasts, a president motivated by a desire to be reelected (and presidents tend to be so motivated)
will have an incentive to create an inferior (from the perspective of the
electorate) policy.[9]

But the alternative of monitoring (and voting on the basis of) policies
rather than outcomes may lead to worse results. Incumbents will have an
incentive to overstate the quality of their policies and to blame their bad
outcomes on bad luck, their predecessor's incompetence, or the Federal
Reserve Board. Given the complexity of economic policy-making, it will
always be possible for incumbents to do this, and it will always be difficult
for voters to discern whether these claims have merit. It may be foolish
for voters to ask whether they are better off now than they were four
years ago, but at least voters can know the answer to that question. The
alternative, to ask whether policies were good over the last four years,
may have no ascertainable answer, and may simply give incumbents incentives to dissemble.

Consider the elections in 1980 and 1984. In his debate with Jimmy
Carter a week before the 1980 election, Ronald Reagan said: "[Carter] has
blamed the people for inflation, OPEC, he's blamed the Federal Reserve
System, he has blamed the lack of productivity of the American people.
. . . We have inflation because the government is living too well." One
might quarrel with Reagan's view of the cause of inflation, or Carter's
view, but one could not quarrel with the fact of high inflation in 1980.

In 1984 Walter Mondale did not deny that the economy had performed
relatively well in the past year. Rather, he attributed that good performance to shortsighted policy (deficit finance) for which the piper was
eventually going to have to be paid (increased taxes). But voters appeared
to look at economic performance in 1984 and not which candidate was
fibbing about whether taxes would have to be raised in 1985. Again,
reasonable people could differ over long-term American economic pros-
pects but most people would have had little trouble agreeing that the
economy had performed relatively well in 1984. It does not seem reasonable to argue that elections ought to turn on debates over the speculations
of economists, especially when those speculations differ and often turn
out to have nothing to do with what eventually comes to pass.

Given the difficulty of monitoring and evaluating past policy, perhaps
voters should try to look at predictions about future outcomes. These

predictions are available and may provide as much information about the incumbent as examination of his policies and with less risk. After all, why do we care about policies? Because we have some feeling that good policies now will lead to good outcomes now and in the future, but that good outcomes now may be produced by inferior (or lucky) policies.

But even this strategy makes too many assumptions about our knowledge of macroeconomics. Can voters believe the economic forecasts they see? What should they do when there are diverse forecasts? How are ordinary voters to evaluate the qualifications of the forecasters?[10] Is it worth their while to even spend the time learning about those forecasts? The principal-agent approach to elections suggests negative answers to those questions. Thus it may make sense for voters to behave in an extremely naive manner; naivete is not equivalent to stupidity.

It is difficult to say more about how the electorate should behave to keep their leaders from shirking. We can say more about how actual electorates do behave, that is, what incentives they give their leaders (assuming their leaders desire reelection). I shall deal with this question for the remainder of this essay in the context of United States presidential elections. It is easiest to look at incentives for economic policy-making, and I limit myself to that arena.[11] We can either look at what incentives are provided, or whether the electorate seems to behave as a "sensible" principal. I shall do both.

WHAT DOES THE ELECTORATE WANT?

Ideally I would like to use evidence based on voting decisions to study these questions. Unfortunately the voting studies that have been done do not contain a rich enough set of questions for this purpose. The alternative is to use public opinion data on approval of the president. For almost every month there is a measure of how much the public approves presidential job performance. This approval measure is often called "presidential popularity" and I shall use approval and popularity synonymously. There are also monthly measures of economic outcomes, policy, and forecasts.[12]

Use of approval scores imposes two important limitations. First, strictly speaking, I can only look at elections in which voters control their leaders via referendum (retrospective)-type elections. This is because the approval ratings only give us the voters' evaluations of the incumbent, not the challenger. But presumably more approved presidents are more likely to defeat any challenger, no matter what voting rule is used. Second, by looking at overall approval I will ignore differences in approval between groups. While much modern research (such as Hibbs 1987, or Kernell 1986) does look at approval by group or party, we can get a simpler understanding of incentives by looking only at overall approval ratings.

Presidents also can use public approval as a resource (Neustadt 1960). As Kernell (1986) has shown, recent presidents have made much more use of public opinion. Thus it is of interest to know what types of presidential actions can lead to public approval. If presidents need approval, then the public can sanction presidents by withholding that approval. Presidential approval is of interest in its own right as well as in its role as a surrogate for electoral decisions. What then is the relationship of the economy to presidential approval?

There are many indicators of how well the economy is doing. These measures are often interrelated. There are, in addition, many noneconomic causes of popularity. To study the effect of one economic variable on popularity while holding other effects on popularity "constant," we must use a a technique called "multiple regression." Multiple regression is the political scientist's attempt to deal with the fact that while we cannot do experiments we do want to know the effect of one variable on another, holding other variables constant. The technique tells us, for example, the effect of a 1-point increase in unemployment on popularity, holding constant the rate of inflation. Other variables which might affect popularity are also (statistically) held constant; this is to eliminate the effects on popularity of such events as Watergate and Vietnam. For more complete results and technical details the reader should consult the various original works whose results are used here.[13]

While I am only presenting a sketch of results here, the reader must be aware of several seemingly technical issues to correctly interpret the findings. First, many results differ because of different things being held constant. Unemployment may seem to have a large impact on popularity, but that impact may disappear if growth of the economy is held constant. This is because the two indicators are highly related, so if growth of the economy is held constant unemployment cannot vary very much. Since most analysts tend to hold different things constant, this makes it very hard to compare their results.

In addition, we would not expect changes in the economy to affect popularity instantaneously. A 1-point increase in inflation might lower popularity somewhat this month. If that increase disappears next month, people might still remember that increase and continue to punish the president for a while. If the price increase persists, its full effect on popularity might not be felt for several years. This means that the economy may have a small effect on monthly popularity, but over time that effect may become quite substantial. Thus it is very important to look at the dynamic properties of the various models. This gets us into very technical questions, and again different researchers deal with this issue in different ways. The interested reader is referred to the technical works cited above; for the purposes of this essay it merely is necessary to remember that there are long- as well as short-run consequences of the economy. With these difficulties in mind, let us turn to some actual political analysis.

HOW MUCH INFLATION WILL THE ELECTORATE TOLERATE?

Economists distinguish between "real" and "nominal" economic variables. The latter are measured in current dollars, and hence are heavily influenced by the rate of inflation. "Real" variables are in constant dollars, and thus measure how well the economy is actually performing. We can distinguish between that portion of economic performance due to inflation (the "nominal" component) and that portion due to actual economic change (the "real" component). The "real" component affects how well off people actually are, whereas the "nominal" component simply tells people what prices they face.

It is easy to measure the costs of "real" changes in the economy, such as increased unemployment or declining real per capita personal income. It is much harder to measure the costs of inflation. Indeed economists have great difficulty in telling whether there are costs to a high (say 10 percent), but constant, rate of inflation.[14] Hibbs (1987, chapter 3) has gone to great lengths to document the economic costs of unemployment. Citing a wide range of types of evidence he clearly shows the costs of unemployment to the American economy, and particularly to the American worker.

Hibbs finds it much more difficult to document the costs of inflation.

Nobody thinks that inflation is a good thing, but it is hard to find good economic evidence of just how bad inflation is. In particular, it is very hard to find any evidence that one more point of inflation is more costly than one more point of unemployment, while Hibbs has no difficulty finding evidence in the opposite direction. Inflation may be more costly than unemployment, but the case is very far from being clear-cut.[15]

Of course some people may feel worse off if they face higher prices, even if their "real" situation has not changed. Whether or not it makes economic sense, people may simply dislike inflation, perhaps because it is costly, perhaps because it creates uncertainty, or perhaps because it is a sign of "moral rot." How do voters trade off unemployment for inflation?[16] How much extra unemployment are people willing to put up with in order to lower inflation by one point?

The political system must answer that question all the time. In 1981 and 1982 the answer was that it was worth about 3 extra points of unemployment for almost three years to bring inflation down quickly from about 10 percent to about 4 percent. During the 1976 campaign Jimmy Carter suggested that voters use the "misery index" to evaluate the incumbent. (Carter probably wished in 1980 that he had never mentioned the misery index.) This index, coined by the economist Arthur Okun, is the sum of inflation and unemployment. The implicit assumption behind the misery index is that a point of inflation is as bad as a point of unemployment. By this standard the economy was performing much better in 1982 than in 1980 (a misery index of 13.6 as compared to 20.2), although it is far from obvious that people were "better off" in 1982 than in 1980.

But was the Reagan anti-inflationary policy what the voters wanted? If a president makes policy to minimize the misery index, is he doing what the electorate wants? It seems that, contrary to economic logic, the American electorate is more worried about inflation than unemployment. Hibbs, for example, finds that the electorate regards an extra point of inflation to be as costly as about 1.5 more points of unemployment. He finds that Democrats have a one-to-one tradeoff between unemployment and inflation, but Republicans and independents find a point of extra inflation to be twice as serious as an extra point of unemployment. An extra 2 points of unemployment will decrease presidential approval by a bit more than 3 points in a year and about 5.5 points eventually. A similar increase in inflation would decrease approval by about 4.5 points within a year and about 8 points eventually.[17]

My research finds that voters are about equally sensitive to high unemployment or inflation. They do, in addition, penalize the president for increases in the unemployment rate. While the size of the penalty for increasing unemployment is large, the unemployment rate is fairly stable from month to month, so it is the overall level of unemployment that is the principal determinant of presidential popularity. A 0.2-point monthly increase in unemployment, which is large, would decrease approval by about 1 point. Near double-digit unemployment, which we saw in the early 1980s, decreases approval by about 2 percent per month; double-digit inflation, seen in the late 1970s, has a similar impact on approval.

The asymmetry in the evaluation of unemployment and inflation has consequences for the timing of policy. Presidential approval declines more quickly at the beginning of a steep recession, and, conversely, improves more quickly with a return to good times.[18] Presidents can take advantage of this by creating political business cycles. If these cycles are characterized by declining unemployment in the months before an election, this strategy will aid the president, even if the preelection boom also features increased inflation before the election.

In the long run it appears as though the "misery index" is a good indicator of the political costs of unemployment and inflation. It may slightly understate the political costs of inflation, as Hibbs found, or it may be quite accurate, as I found. But in any event it is not too far wrong. This is the case in spite of the possible difference in the economic costs of inflation and unemployment.

It is interesting to see how these findings compare to those in other countries. In the United States, voters punish incumbents for not providing price stability. Other electorates do not appear to be as inflation averse. Hibbs (1985) finds that in the United States a 2-point increase in inflation leads to a 6-point decrease in approval; a similar figure for Germany is a bit under 2 points, and for Sweden is only 0.5 points. Americans, on the other hand, punish their leaders less for high rates of unemployment, with the British punishing their leaders 50 percent more and the Swedes punishing their leaders almost three times as much. Why have American presidents pursued policies that lead to comparatively high unemployment but comparative price stability? The answer from a principal-agent perspective is that presidents as agents are simply doing what their principals, the electorate, want them to do.[19]

THE TIME FRAME OF THE ELECTORATE

The question of the relative electoral costs of unemployment and inflation is the simplest question we can look at in the principal-agent framework. A second question relates to the memory of the electorate. How quickly does the electorate reward or punish sustained changes in economic performance? How quickly does the electorate forget past performance? If voters forget the past quickly there is no reason for a president early in his term to worry about what the electorate wants. If it takes a long time for economic success to show up as increased approval, then manipulations near election day will have little payoff. Does this seem to be the case?

We can measure the memory of the electorate by studying whether a change in the economy in a single quarter affects popularity in subsequent quarters. All three analysts agree that the electorate has a fairly long memory. Something over 80 percent of a previous quarter's effect persists into the next quarter. Consider a temporary downturn in the economy which costs the president one point in his approval rating during the current quarter. In the subsequent quarter this temporary downturn, which has by now disappeared, will still cost him about 0.8 points. This figure will decline to 0.64 the next quarter and so forth. This temporary decline will still cost the president about 0.4 points a year later and almost 0.2 points two years later. Thus the president cannot ignore the electorate's wishes early on in his term and only become attentive to the electorate right before election day.

This long memory also means that sustained changes in the economy can have a fairly large effect on approval, but it will take a long time for this effect to be felt completely. Consider a sustained decrease in inflation. Suppose that it increases popularity by 0.5 points this quarter. But because of memory this quarter's decrease in inflation will increase popularity by 0.4 points next quarter. But next quarter will also have its own lower inflation rate so the total effect next quarter would be a 0.9-point increase in approval. Due to the memory effect, 80 percent of this increase will persist into the next quarter. This will be combined with the direct impact of the lower inflation rate two quarters hence, leading to a total increase in approval of about 1.2 points. This process will continue, with approval continuing to rise due to the sustained improvement in the economy.

Eventually popularity would rise by about 2.5 points, five times its increase in the first quarter.

Hibbs calculates that about 18 percent of the ultimate effect on approval of a sustained change in the economy shows up immediately, with about half the total effect being felt within a year and about 80 percent being achieved within two years and almost all the effect showing up in four years. This means that a president who wishes to satisfy the electorate by making permanent changes in the performance of the economy had better start to do so early in his term if he wishes to reap electoral benefit from those changes. A president making sustained changes in the economy right before an election will find that most of the consequences of that change will show up after election day. If the sustained change is one desired by the electorate the president will thus not reap all the gains from that change; on the other hand, if that change is not a popular one, the president will not suffer all the electoral costs of that change.

This long memory has consequences for political business cycles. In the version of the cycle where the president simply creates a preelection boom, the electorate must respond quickly to the good news of lower unemployment. But we have seen that they respond slowly, with the full effect of a decrease not being felt for several years. Of the increase in approval that a president can generate by lowering unemployment, only half of that increase will show up in one year. Thus, contrary to Tufte, a president should start his electoral manipulation of the economy well before election day. In the more complicated version of the cycle the president must first induce an early-term recession. Theorists, such as Nordhaus, usually assume that voters do not penalize the president very much for this early-term recession. But the finding of long memory means that this is not the case. If voters remember (and punish for) the early-term recession there still may be room for electoral manipulation of the economy, but less room than political business cycle theorists often assume.

HOW SOPHISTICATED IS THE ELECTORATE?

A more interesting question from the perspective of principals and agents is whether the electorate "naively" votes (or approves) on the basis of current outcomes, rather than policy or predictions? If voters are "naive," are they behaving foolishly? In an influential article, Henry Chappell and William Keech (1985) argue that the electorate does and should look at policy as well as outcomes. Such behavior, in particular, would make it fruitless for presidents to try to create political business cycles, since sophisticated voters would see through such chicanery. This argument cuts against the principal-agent perspective which says that it may be too costly or difficult for the electorate to monitor policy.

Of course it is not necessary for voters to monitor outcomes in order for a political business cycle to be of no aid to the president. If voters simply look at forecasts of outcomes, then the forecasted postelection inflation (which we know voters would take seriously) is enough to make the cycle of dubious value. It is possible to forecast outcomes simply on the basis of current and past outcomes. Alec Chrystal and David Peel (1986) argue that the populace makes very sophisticated forecasts about the economy, and then uses those forecasts in evaluating the president. Let me begin with the Chrystal and Peel argument.

Sophisticated actors should use information like any other scarce resource. This insight has led to the movement in economics known as "rational expectations." Chrystal and Peel have applied rational expectations to presidential approval. Much of what voters observe of the current economy could have been predicted based on past outcomes. Current approval should reflect these predictions about future events. For example, if inflation was low last month it is likely to be low this month. If presidents receive full reward for low inflation this month then voters are making a mistake, since their approval last month should have reflected expectations of low inflation this month.

Rational expectations theorists divide today's outcomes into a part that could have been predicted yesterday (the "expected" component) and a part that could not have been forecast based on the information available yesterday (the "unexpected" or "surprise" component). According to rational expectations, only the unexpected part of today's outcomes should affect current popularity since the expected part of today's outcome should already have shown up in yesterday's approval. In fact, it is quite possible for inflation to be lower this month, but higher than it was expected to be. Under those conditions approval should suffer, not gain. If the populace expects increasing inflation after the election, then they will not approve of the president before the election, and hence political business cycles lose their potency.

Is the electorate so rational? If so, approval should look like what is known as a "random walk," that is, changes in approval from month to month should be unforecastable. Thus it should be impossible to make predictions about changing levels of popularity now based on any past information, since that past information should already have been completely used in prior assessments of the president. Only new (that is unforecastable) information can change current levels of approval. This turns out not to be the case. My research shows that we can forecast changes in current popularity. Hence the populace could not have used all the information available last quarter in making its assessment of the president last quarter.

We can break current inflation and unemployment down into its expected and surprise components. If the rational expectations view is correct, then only the surprise component should affect popularity. This turns out not to be the case. The expected component of unemployment or inflation drives current approval just as much (if not more) than the surprise component does. Thus presidential approval is not consistent with rational expectations. Voters do not make rational forecasts about the future economy and use those forecasts in deciding on current approval. This may be because the populace is not very good at making these forecasts, or because they do not believe the forecasts they see. Like Harry Truman, they may wait for the appearance of a one-armed economist, and wait in vain.[20] This finding is quite consistent with the principal-agent perspective on elections: it is simply too costly or difficult for the electorate to obtain good forecasts.

Voters may not look at forecasts of future outcomes but they may still monitor current policy as well as current outcomes. This too would defeat the political business cycle. Unlike forecasts, some measures of policy are observable. This is the argument of Chappell and Keech. They claim that voters accept the idea of there being a natural rate of unemployment.[21] In this perspective if inflation is high it can only be reduced by having an unemployment level above its natural rate. Chappel and Keech then argue that for a given level of inflation last quarter there is a best level of unemployment this quarter. This level may be high, if inflation was high, or low, if inflation was low. But in any event, voters, having some understanding of economics, look at whether economic policy was "correctly" tight or "correctly" easy. Note that all that voters need to know are the observable outcomes—unemployment and inflation—and the economic construct—the natural rate of unemployment. If Chappell and Keech were asking voters to monitor more complicated policy instruments, such as the growth rate of the money supply or the adjusted federal deficit, then we would dismiss their vote as being totally inconsistent with the principal-agent approach. But the strategy for voters that Chappell and Keech suggest appears feasible.

The Chappell and Keech view seems reasonable. Why should voters be so naive as to ignore policy and only look at current outcomes? But sophistication implies a willingness to devote enough resources for the voter to have at least a rudimentary knowledge of economics. If the populace is as Chappell and Keech describe it, then voters must not only look at outcomes but they also must understand the relationship between those outcomes, that is, they must have an economic theory. One merit of the Chappell and Keech approach is that it does not ask voters to observe things that are difficult to observe; the Chappell and Keech voter must observe no more than the simple retrospective voter. But the Chappell and Keech voter must interpret those outcomes.

Should voters believe the idea of a "natural rate of unemployment"? In the absence of our one-armed economist the answer to this question is at best unclear. Even if voters should clearly accept this idea, what is the natural rate? This is a theoretical construct. Imagine the campaign of 1984 fought along the lines that Chappell and Keech suggest. Mondale would have argued that unemployment was too high given the rate of inflation that prevailed in the early 1980s. Reagan's counter might well have been that Mondale had underestimated the natural rate of unemployment (something that liberal and conservative economists seem to disagree about). We would have had a campaign based on whose theoretical constructs seemed superior. Such an issue should hardly be settled by election, and it seemed dubious as to whether elections should turn on such an issue.

The principal-agent view of elections tells us that naivete may well be a very reasonable position for voters to take. It is still an empirical question as to whether the voters are naive or sophisticated in the Chappell and Keech sense. It turns out to be hard to distinguish the Chappell and Keech perspective from the "naive" perspective on purely empirical grounds. This is because both theories have voters monitoring the same set of outcomes, differing only in how voters use those outcomes. My research shows that the naive model fits the data slightly better than does the Chappell and Keech sophisticated model. Voters may well be naive. While this makes sense from the voters' perspective, this does mean that presidents may well have an incentive to create political business cycles.

WHAT OUTCOMES DO VOTERS MONITOR?

If voters monitor outcomes, which ones do they look at? Some economic indicators, such as the growth in real per capita income, are clearly superior. But unfortunately these superior indicators are often very complicated and not easy to observe. Inferior indicators, such as the unemployment rate, are much easier to observe and to understand. The unemployment rate is often the lead story on the TV news and in the local press; stories about real per capita income growth are much more rare outside of the rarified atmosphere of the *Wall Street Journal*.

Similarly there are many different measures of inflation. The best is probably some sophisticated measure based on the National Income and Product Accounts and easily available to all voters who carefully read the financial section of the *New York Times*. Inferior measures, such as the well-known one based on the consumer price index are available to anyone troubling to turn on the nightly news. Even more inferior measures, such as the rate of inflation in local food prices, are available to anyone who goes grocery shopping.

I have looked at a variety of economic predictors of approval, ranging from those that are sophisticated but difficult to observe to those that are easy to observe if less than ideal. I have found that, in general, the simpler measures are better predictors of approval. Thus, for example, the best price predictor of approval is the increase in food and housing prices, while the most sophisticated National Income and Product Account measures predict approval least well. The increase in the producer price index is a better measure of inflation than is a similar measure based on the consumer price index, and the producer price index is surely a better forecaster of future inflation of any kind. But the consumer price index is more readily available (being reported now on the nightly television news), and it also turns out to be a better predictor of presidential approval.

Turning to indicators of the "real" economy, unemployment is probably the least useful measure. Among other things, it is a lagging indicator, reflecting past events rather than predicting future ones. But again, an inferior economic measure is the best political measure. Unemployment is much more closely related to approval than are the superior economic measures based on the growth of real gross national product or real per capita disposable personal income. This is all in accord with the principal-agent perspective on costly monitoring.

Hibbs has suggested that voters should not hold the president accountable for that portion of the economic woes of the 1970s due to OPEC oil price increases. Presumably these price increases were beyond the president's control. This is in direct conflict with the principal-agent approach, which says that it is too difficult for voters to discern the causes of their economic woes. Should not the voters also discount for bad weather leading to bad harvests? Imagine an election hinging on whether rainfall was below normal? Was the success of the OPEC cartel in 1973 not directly due to Henry Kissinger's Middle Eastern policy? Voters and politicians could argue about the answer to the latter question, but no one could question that the 1970s were not the best of times. From the perspective of principal and agent it is only the latter that is of relevance. Empirically I have not found any tendency for voters to blame the president less for that portion of the difficulties of the 1970s that might be attributed to the OPEC cartel.[22]

CONCLUSIONS

We can think of the president and the electorate as being in a relationship of agent and principal. Thinking this way gives us insight into the behavior of both the president and the electorate. The basic question for the president is how can he do what he wants while still making sure that he can be reelected; the basic question for voters is how they can monitor presidential behavior without expending too much time or effort.

One of the recurring debates in political science is whether voters are sophisticated or naive. It is typically assumed that sophistication is superior to naivete. From the principal-agent perspective naivete may well be a reasonable strategy for many voters. It makes sense, from this perspective, for voters to judge the president based on observed economic outcomes rather than imputed economic policy, and it appears that voters do judge the president in this way. It also makes sense for voters to use easily available and understandable economic indicators, and they do appear to use such indicators even when economists know that better indicators are available.

Presidents can take advantage of such simplified judgments by the electorate. They can make economic policy that has long-term bad consequences but produces good outcomes now. In particular they can produce a boom before election day, even if that boom will have bad inflationary consequences later. But the long memory of the electorate will penalize the president for an early-term recession, so there is some limit on how effective the strategy of inducing a political business cycle can be.

Elections cannot be fought on potential problems, and presidents can take advantage of this. Presidents have an incentive to produce good outcomes now even if this will have bad long-term economic consequences. There is little incentive for presidents to offer the populace unpleasant medicine, unless they can reap the fruits of economic health well before election day. Republican presidents, whose natural tendency is to offer harsh medicine to fight inflation, must be aware of this problem.

Insider accounts of presidential policy-making in the Nixon and Reagan administrations go into great detail about creative solutions to this problem.[23] The Nixon administration was unwilling to fight inflation with a recession; instead we got the cosmetic solution of wage and price controls. Price increases were merely postponed from 1971 to 1973, but inflation was low in November of 1972. The Reagan solution to fighting inflation without pain was supply side economics. When it turned out that inflation could not be eliminated painlessly the Reagan administration had the political sense to make sure that pain would be inflicted during the early part of the administration, with the benefits reaped well before election day. In 1984 Reagan benefited greatly from the asymmetric way which voters judge unemployment and inflation. While unemployment was high in 1984, it had fallen dramatically over the previous year, and voters appear to care as much about changes in the unemployment rate as its level. Inflation, on the other hand, was low in 1984, but not falling. Fortunately for Reagan, voters appear to care about the absolute level of inflation, not its rate of change.

Finally, presidents who want to be reelected must do, more or less, what the electorate wants. This is the case even if what the electorate wants appears foolish to the analyst. The electorate appears to regard inflation as at least as a serious problem, and perhaps more so, than is unemployment, in spite of the difficulty economists have in assessing the costs of inflation. But even though the misery index may overstate the true costs of inflation, it accurately states its political costs. When we ask why the United States was recently willing to bear such incredible costs to bring down the inflation rate quickly, one compelling answer is that it was because the electorate wanted this done (and that presidents who want to get reelected had better worry about what the voters want).

NOTES

1. For the purposes of this chapter I will assume that presidents are always able to run for reelection. This has not been true since the passage of the Twenty-Second Amendment. I will assume that second-term presidents are eager to have their party continue to hold the White House. Such an assumption may not be completely accurate, but it is a reasonable first cut. For the time period under study here (1953–1988), only Eisenhower and Reagan were in a position to make policy when they were legally ineligible for reelection.

2. See Fiorina (1981) for the clearest statement of this position.

3. A good introduction to this literature from the standpoint of political science is Moe (1984).

4. There are costs to this reneging. Election efforts demand strong efforts by loyal supporters. Failure to keep promises will erode this loyalty. Hibbs (1977, 1987) assumes that this is the critical mechanism in American politics. Presidents represent core groups and, once in office, simply do whatever their core groups desire. Hence there is no problem of agency for Hibbs.

My view (Beck 1982) is that presidents have more flexibility than this. They must make appeals outside their core group, and so they cannot always keep their promises. It is clearly the case that presidential campaigns are won both with the loyalty of a party's core group of supporters and by making appeals to supporters of the other party. More complicated theories would take account of both of these aspects of campaigns, but for my purposes here I ignore the question of loyalty. Presidents clearly make commitments during a campaign, and there are costs to them for reneging on those promises. The principal-agent approach more or less ignores those costs, since voters are assumed to discount any promises.

Alt (1985) has recently come up with a clever way of synthesizing the two positions. Early on in a term presidents will keep their promises, both because voters will remember those promises and because presidents want to build up their credibility. Later on, as voters forget and presidents are already credible, presidents can start making policy with their eye on the next election, that is, they can start making appeals to nonsupporters. Alt has found some empirical confirmation for his position.

5. We often assume that the Carter years were an economic disaster. While

inflation and unemployment were high in 1979 and 1980, Carter's performance was not all that awful when compared with Reagan's. Carter's flaw was high inflation, and it is not clear how to measure the costs of inflation. If economic performance is measured by real personal income per capita, Carter performed only slightly worse than did Reagan. Real income grew about 6 percent under Carter and grew a bit over 7 percent during the first Reagan term. Performance under either of these presidents was worse than during the 1960s, where income grew about 14 percent over 4 years, but better than for the period 1973–1976, when it grew only 4 percent. Income growth returned to its 1960s' robustness in the early part of the second Reagan administration, although performance has been more lackluster recently. In any event the Carter years were not the economic disaster we often remember them to be have been.

6. This situation may describe the recent Thatcher reelections in the U.K. While the overall performance of the British economy has not been terrific, those who are employed do quite well. Unfortunately there is now a more or less permanently unemployed group of former industrial workers in the north of England. Mrs. Thatcher appears to get a large majority of the votes of those who are doing well (the employed in the south) and few of the votes of those who are doing poorly (the unemployed). Because British voters seem to be voting on the basis of their personal outcomes, Mrs. Thatcher does not have to attempt to make policy to deal with the depressed north.

7. See Kiewiet (1983) and the references cited there. The term *sociotropic* was coined by Kiewiet's frequent collaborator, Donald Kinder.

8. See Popkin et al. (1976) for a good discussion of the costs of obtaining information for voters for whom elections are not very important. Popkin calls his theory one of "investment voting" and is based on Downs's (1957) seminal work. Much of the principal-agent perspective on monitoring cost is similar to that of "investment voting." Only the principal-agent perspective focuses on the informational advantages of the president, and his ability to use that advantage for his own (electoral) purposes. The problem for the voter is not merely costly information but also the inability to monitor policy-making. Popkin et al. focus only on the former problem.

9. The initial work on the political business cycle was that of William Nordhaus (1975). Edward Tufte (1978) popularized the Nordhaus model. Nordhaus is associated with manipulation over the entire term, whereas Tufte stresses the preelection boom part of the cycle without the early term recession.

10. Studies of economic forecasting find that forecasters do relatively well in normal times but have great difficulty in predicting turns in the business cycle and in making predictions given unprecedented events (OPEC price increases, huge deficits). Of course, it is exactly under those circumstances that forecasts will be of most use for the voter. See, for example, McNees and Ries (1983).

11. The analysis could be extended to other arenas. For example, should presi-

dents who wish to be reelected engage in foreign affairs? But presidents cannot manipulate foreign policy in the way they can economic policy, and so the question for strategic electorally motivated presidents is most interesting in the economic policy arena. For some arenas the analysis might be vacuous, leading to such pronouncements as do not get caught in a Watergate- or Irangate-type situation.

12. Approval is measured by the Gallup organization. End-of-the-month surveys are used here, and figures are interpolated for months with no survey. Approval is measured by the percent of the sample who respond "approve" to the question "Do you approve or disapprove of the way —— is handling his job as president." Details on measurement can be found in Beck (1987) or Hibbs (1987). Hibbs (1987, p. 142) cites many references that show a strong relationship between a president's approval rating and his success at the next election.

13. My technical discussion is in Beck (1987). Hibbs (1987, chapter 5) contains an extensive discussion on popularity functions. Chappell and Keech (1985) also have a long and useful discussion. In this paper I more or less limit myself to the results in those papers or books, although there are many other useful studies. When I reference Hibbs, Chappell and Keech, or my work without specific citation, I refer to those particular works.

14. When I speak of high inflation I do so in the U.S. context, meaning low double-digit inflation. Obviously "Latin" inflation of 20–30 percent or hypernflation of over 100 percent is a very serious problem, but there is no evience that double-digit inflation leads to Latin or hyperinflation. See Maier (1978).

15. Barry (1985) also has a nice discussion of whether inflation really is a serious problem. His claim is that economists' obsession with inflation is ideological. It should be stressed again that this position has neither been shown to be true or false.

16. There are many better measures of the real economy than unemployment, such as the growth in per capita GNP or the growth in per capita real personal income, but politically the most talked about real measure is the unemployment rate. For now I measure inflation as the rate of change in the consumer price index. Again, there are many superior measures of inflation (based on the National Income and Product Accounts), but the consumer price measure seems to be politically most relevant. I return to the question of alternative measures below, and show why, in a principal-agent context, it makes sense for voters to use these inferior measures.

17. Chappell and Keech find an even more inflationary-averse population. Their "sophisticated" voters faced with a 10 percent inflation rate would like a severe depression (output 19 percent below its potential; in the depths of the 1981–1982 recession, output was never more than 10 percent below its potential). Their "naive" voters do not punish the president at all for unemployment (there

is a slight, but statistically insignificant, increase in popularity with increased unemployment). It should be noted that this preference may well be for a very short recession, since such a drop in output should quickly dampen inflationary expectations.

18. Unemployment is a lagging economic indicator. Businesses wait until a recession is well under way before laying off workers, but wait to make sure that a recovery is real before rehiring those workers. For example, the economy began to recover in late 1982 but unemployment did not decline until well into 1983. Thus the decline in popularity will start after the technical onset of a recession, and will improve after the technical end of a recession. Recessions are officially dated by the National Bureau for Economic Research on the basis of real growth in the gross national product.

19. This approach does not explain why the electorate wants what it wants. Political leaders certainly educate the public. Thus Ronald Reagan may have been an important factor in educating the public about the dangers of inflation. But having educated the electorate, he then was forced to live with the consequences of that education.

20. President Truman was reported to have expressed annoyance at all his economic advice being prefaced with "on the one hand" or "but on the other hand."

21. This claim is that there is a fixed underlying rate of unemployment in the economy. This natural rate is determined by the structure of the economy (training of the work force, international competetiveness, age of capital stock, and so forth) and not by government policy. Government policy can cause unemployment to be above or below its natural rate temporarily, but eventually unemployment cannot deviate from its natural rate. If unemployment is temporarily above its natural rate the rate of inflation will decrease, but if it is under its natural rate the rate of inflation will increase. Thus it is bad for unemployment to be below its natural rate for very long (because unemployment will inevitably return to its natural rate but with higher inflation) but it may be moved above its natural rate for short periods of time to reduce inflation. While this is the model of the economy that Chappell and Keech subscribe to, not all economists accept this position.

22. Hibbs reaches the opposite conclusion. For technical reasons it is impossible to assess the variability of his estimates, so it is impossible to know how to assess this particular finding.

23. See Stein (1984) for a good discussion of economic policy-making in both the Nixon and early Reagan administrations. Greider (1987) provides a good account of economic policy-making in the Reagan administration.

REFERENCES

Alt, J. (1985). Political parties, world demand and unemployment: domestic and international sources of economic activity. *American Political Science Review* 79:1016–40.

Barry, B. (1985). Does democracy cause inflation? Political ideas of some economists. In Lindberg, L. and Maier, C. (eds.). *The Politics of Inflation and Economic Stagflation*. Washington, D.C.: Brookings Institution.

Beck, N. (1982). Parties, administrations and macroeconomic outcomes. *American Political Science Review* 76:83–93.

———. (1987). The economy and presidential popularity: An attempt at a rational model and improved econometric estimates. Paper prepared for a conference on "Economics and Elections in the United States and Western Europe," Bellagio, Italy, May 4–9.

Chappell, H., and Keech, W. (1985). A new view of political accountability for economic performance. *American Political Science Review* 79:10–27.

Chrystal, K. A., and Peel, D. (1986). What can economists learn from political science and vice versa? *American Economic Review* 76(2): 62–65.

Downs, A. (1957). *An Economic Theory of Democracy*. New York: Harper and Row.

The Federalist Papers. See Hamilton, A., Madison, J., and Jay, J.

Ferejohn, J. (1986). Incumbent performance and electoral control. *Public Choice* 50:5–25.

Fiorina, M. (1981). *Retrospective Voting in American National Elections*. New Haven: Yale University Press.

Greider, W. (1987). *Secrets of the Temple: How the Federal Reserve Runs the Country*. New York: Simon & Schuster.

Hamilton, A., Madison, J., and Jay, J. ([1787–88] 1961). *The Federalist Papers*, edited by Clinton Rossiter. New York: New American Library.

Hibbs, D. (1977). Political parties and macroeconomic policy. *American Political Science Review* 71:1467–87.

———. (1985). Inflation, political support and macroeconomic policy. In Lindberg, L. and Maier, C. (eds.). *The Politics of Inflation and Economic Stagflation*. Washington, D.C.: Brookings Institution.

———. (1987). *The American Political Economy: Macroeconomics and Electoral Politics in the United States*. Cambridge: Harvard University Press.

Kernell, S. (1986). *Going Public: New Strategies of Presidential Leadership*. Washington, D.C.: CQ Press.

Kiewiet, D. (1983). *Macroeconomics and Micropolitics*. Chicago: University of Chicago Press.

McNees, S., and Ries, J. (1983). The track record of macroeconomic forecasts. *New England Economic Review* November: 5–18.

Maier, C. (1978). The politics of inflation in the twentieth century. In Hirsch, F. and Goldthorpe, J. (eds.). *The Political Economy of Inflation*. Cambridge: Harvard University Press.

Moe, T. (1984). The new economics of organization. *American Journal Political Science* 28:739–77.

Neustadt, R. (1960). *Presidential Power*. New York: Wiley.

Nordhaus, W. (1975). The political business cycle. *Review of Economic Studies* 42:169–90.

Popkin, S., Gorman, J., Phillips, C., and Smith, J. (1976). What have you done for me lately? Toward an investment theory of voting. *American Political Science Review* 70:779–805.

Stein, H. (1984). *Presidential Economics*. New York: Simon & Schuster.

Tufte, E. (1978). *Political Control of the Economy*. Princeton: Princeton University Press.

SEVEN

Secrecy and Spectacle: Reflections on the Dangers of the Presidency

Bruce Miroff

The presidency is, simultaneously, the most visible and the most hidden of American political institutions. It is the most visible because one man is easier to watch than a plurality of actors, and because that one man now receives an enormous amount of media attention. It is the most hidden because an individual is more able to keep secrets than a plurality, and because that individual now enjoys enormous capacities to control and manipulate secret information.

The seeming paradox of a visible/hidden presidency has been present from the beginning of our constitutional order. In *Federalist* No. 70, the classic argument for a strong and energetic executive, Alexander Hamilton assured readers with unhappy memories of the British crown that a unitary American executive would be safe. This executive, Hamilton insisted, could be held accountable because he was so visible; in his words, "one man, . . . from the very circumstance of his being alone, will be more narrowly watched and more readily suspected." But Hamilton hardly wanted everything the president undertook to be transparent to the public gaze. Earlier in *Federalist* No. 70, he had suggested that unity in the

I wish to thank Melinda Lawson, James Miller, and Todd Swanstrom for their helpful comments.

presidency contributed to executive energy because it fostered not only decisiveness and dispatch, but "secrecy" as well.[1]

If the president has been both highly visible and specially secretive from the start, both of these qualities have grown stronger in the modern presidency. They have, I will argue, also grown more dangerous. The enhanced visibility of the modern president is obvious if we survey the modern media. A vast press corps now follows a president everywhere he goes, chronicling deeds and words, and reporting even the most trivial of presidential habits. On the front page, in the lead story, at the top of the nightly news, the president is customarily the center of focus. The enhanced secrecy of the modern presidency, if less apparent to the casual observer, is easily evident to the careful inquirer. The president sits atop what has been called "an invisible government," with covert agencies available to do his bidding and classification systems available to keep the results concealed. In occasional moments of forced revelation, we have the opportunity to peer through what is normally an impenetrable veil of secrecy.

I will first consider presidential secrecy, and then presidential visibility (in a form I will call "spectacle"), in separate discussions. But the central point of this chapter is the dangerous interconnection of secrecy and spectacle in the modern presidency. Secrecy and spectacle have come to feed off each other. Two faces of a modern president, a hidden face and a public face, thus come to be merged as a false face. This false face, I will suggest, should even trouble those whose primary concern is presidential power and success. It should especially worry those who care about the accountability of presidents and the quality of American democracy.

Let us consider secrecy first. The extensive apparatus of executive secrecy that has been created since World War II has been justified by the exigencies of global responsibility and the cold war. No one questions the idea that some secrets must be kept—for example, about precarious diplomatic negotiations or the technical details of weapons systems. But what the revelations of the mid-1970s and more recently of the Iran-Contra affair have pointed to is a realm of secrecy that not only undermines presidential accountability and sabotages public judgment, but that even damages the presidency itself.

Secret action is seductive for the presidency. It offers a president the opportunity to advance his foreign policy goals with methods of actions that would raise ethical as well as constitutional problems if openly pursued. It permits a president to persist in a course of policy even if that policy lacks support from, or is strongly opposed by, majorities in congress and among the American people. The Reagan administration's decision to form a counterrevolutionary force against the Nicaraguan government illustrates the first of these temptations of secret action; the financing and arming of this force in the face of a congressional prohibition illustrates the second. But secret action often turns out to entail hidden costs. The report of the Tower commission, when added to the revelations of Nixon's plumbers' unit, CIA assassination plots, and the like, suggests the proposition that secrecy engenders folly. The Tower Commission tells a familiar sad story, of a small group of men in the White House, obsessed with secrecy, but managing in the end less to keep others in the dark than to create their own darkness. These men were made foolish because they could not test reality; their secretiveness prevented them from consulting diverse and expert sources, and from subjecting their projects to independent external review. These men were made foolish because they did not have to answer for their ideas; the necessity of justification that is characteristic of policies advanced publicly, that makes officials think through the arguments, implications, and consequences of what they wish to do, is eliminated in the realm of covert action. Many examples might be cited from the Tower Commission Report to illustrate the self-created mental darkness of secret operatives in the executive. My favorite is an almost plaintive statement from Oliver North, in a memo to National Security Adviser John Poindexter about coordinating efforts to solicit money for the Contras from foreign heads of state: "At this point I'm not sure who on our side knows what. Help."[2]

Secrecy also encourages contempt for democratic procedures and democratic values. Secret actors in the executive branch justify their deeds with references to foreign enemies. But in private, they express a scorn for the American public, a disdain for congress, a disinterest in legality that they would never dare to articulate openly. In private, they depict themselves as superior to the requirements of democracy, whether abroad or at home. In a secret meeting, Henry Kissinger explains why the United States should intervene to prevent the democratic election of Salvador Allende in Chile: "I don't see why we need to stand by and watch a country go Communist due to the irresponsibility of its own people."[3] In a secret memo, Oliver North informs Admiral Poindexter that he has appeared before the House Intelligence Committee and told them that he knows nothing of Contra military operations; Poindexter's response to this egregious falsehood is "Well done."[4] The same words are used by

Poindexter's predecessor, Robert McFarlane, to praise North's covert activities. McFarlane goes on to tell North: "If the world only knew how many times you have kept a semblance of integrity and gumption in U.S. policy, they would make you Secretary of State. But they can't know and would complain if they did—such is the state of democracy in the late 20th century."[5]

Nowhere is the immense problem that secrecy presents for presidential accountability—and also presidential rationality—more evident than in our experience with the strange doctrine of "plausible deniability." This doctrine holds that presidents should be sufficiently insulated from detailed knowledge of a covert operation so that they can plausibly deny their own involvement should the operation embarrassingly come to light. It aims to let presidents have it both ways: to control a powerful instrument for the secret implementation of some of their foreign policy goals, yet to escape responsibility if their agents' misdeeds are exposed.

"Plausible deniability" makes it terribly difficult, even after many years, to pin down just what presidents have done in the realm of the covert. A remarkable instance of this is the question of John F. Kennedy's role in CIA assassination plots aimed at the charismatic leader of Cuba, Fidel Castro. Was the CIA, in its repeated blundering efforts to murder Castro, operating with the authority of the president? This was a question that the Senate's Church Committee, investigating CIA misdeeds in 1975, never could answer to satisfactorily.

When asked by the Church Committee as to whether President Kennedy could have authorized covert plots against Castro's life, Kennedy's top foreign policy advisers, such as Assistant for National Security Affairs McGeorge Bundy and Secretary of Defense Robert McNamara, said no. These Kennedy intimates testified that the president had never spoken of such a matter to them. Further, they insisted that assassination as a means of carrying out presidential policy was totally foreign to Kennedy's character, beliefs, and values. At the same time, they insisted that the CIA under Kennedy had been a disciplined organization that would not undertake major actions without proper authorization. The resulting paradox was obvious: Kennedy could not, according to the testimony, have ordered an assassination, and the CIA would not have acted without his authorization, but the CIA had nonetheless tried to kill Fidel Castro. Kennedy's men could respond to this paradox only by expressions of bewilderment and mystification.

The CIA officials involved in the Castro assassination plots cast the story in a different light. They insisted that they had proceeded with proper authorization, and that this authorization came from the president of the United States. They did not claim, however, that President Kennedy had directly ordered, either in writing or verbally, Castro's assassination. Such matters, the CIA's Richard Helms told the Church Committee, were not to be discussed with a president. As Helms explained the CIA perspective: "I just think we all had the feeling that we're hired out to keep these things out of the Oval Office."[6] Kennedy was to be insulated not only from sordid details, but from culpable knowledge. Still, the CIA officials felt that they had his approval. Both the president and his brother, the attorney general, were putting the CIA under intense pressure to bring Castro down. The White House often used phrases such as "get rid of Castro" and "knock off Castro" in communicating with agency officials. In this climate of fierce Kennedy administration hostility to Castro, the CIA felt it had the go-ahead to try any expedient, including murder. Helms's testimony on this point was chillingly matter-of-fact: "I believe it was the policy at the time to get rid of Castro and if killing him was one of the things that was to be done in this connection, that was within what was expected."[7]

The Church committee was stymied by the vague, circumlocutory language of covert action. In the realm of executive secrecy, presidents do not necessarily say what they really mean, and covert operators can read meanings into presidential statements. In this hidden realm, presidents do not have to order illegal actions, and yet illegal actions can be performed by covert operatives under the impression that they have been officially sanctioned. Confronted with this murky situation, as well as with the understandable concern of both Kennedy men and CIA officials to leave the matter clouded, the Church committee could not answer the question of John Kennedy's responsibility for plotting assassination. That the president was kept at a distance from the plots against Castro, that both he and the CIA followed "plausible deniability" to the extent that he did not want to know and the CIA was content to act on the basis that it was carrying out his will, is a scenario that I find believable. On the other hand, it is not hard to argue for a quite different scenario, in which Kennedy appears more directly responsible. Such an argument, built from intriguing fragments of circumstantial evidence, can be found in Thomas Powers's biography of Richard Helms. As Powers states his position: "Lacking a smoking gun in the form of an incriminatory document or personal testimony, we can reach no firm or final conclusion, but at the same time the available evidence leans heavily toward a finding that the Kennedys did, in fact, authorize the CIA to make an attempt on Castro's life."[8]

The Castro assassination plots suggest that "plausible deniability" may undercut not only presidential accountability, but also rational and effective presidential control of subordinates who act in the covert realm. The same lesson is suggested in our most recent encounter with "plausible deniability." The question that came to dominate the congressional investigations of the Iran-Contra affair in the summer of 1987 was whether President Reagan knew of the diversion of profits from arms sales to Iran to the support of the Nicaraguan Contras. The Contra war was, for President Reagan, a holy crusade, and his aides on the National Security Council staff knew the intensity of his will on this subject just as CIA officials had known of the Kennedy brothers' will on the subject of Fidel Castro. Once again, "plausible deniability" became the justification, according to Reagan's national security adviser, John Poindexter, for proceeding covertly to accomplish the president's objective without directly informing the president. In this case, "plausible deniability" protected a sitting president from even greater political damage than he had already suffered, so that it is easy to be even more skeptical than in the case of Kennedy. But the world of secret operatives is so murky and tangled that we cannot be sure, in the absence of harder evidence, one way or the other. Abundant evidence of President Reagan's disengaged managerial style, and of the grandiose amateurism of his covert crew, makes it plausible to suggest that the president did not exactly know what his zealous alter egos were doing.[9] At this point, we are left with a frustrating uncertainty on a matter quite crucial for public judgment.

It is understandable that secrecy has become attractive to most recent presidents. The tools of secret action are largely a modern creation; before the establishment of the CIA in 1947 presidents did not possess the means, at least in peacetime, to carry out extensive clandestine missions abroad. The availability of these tools offers presidents an escape from the reality of international frustrations through covert schemes of manipulation and control. The mushrooming media coverage of the White House in the postwar years has encouraged secrecy in a different sense. A president who makes a practice of openness may find, as did Jimmy Carter, that his political flaws and policy confusions are rapidly broadcast, to his detriment.

But the costs of secrecy need to be considered. Secrecy fosters foolish plots and nurtures contempt for democratic procedures and democratic values. It brings into being a political netherworld in which subordinates pursue assumed mandates over which presidents may lack informed judgment and adequate control. Secrecy has often turned out to be damaging to presidential effectiveness. Its greater costs, however, is to American democracy. The American people cannot judge what they do not know.

Secrecy has created a hidden face of the modern presidency. What the citizenry does see—the president's public face—may also be misleading. Some of the most visible presidential actions do not serve to inform the American people or to facilitate public judgment. On the contrary, their significance lies in their utility to the White House as a spectacle.

Spectacle is a less familiar category then secrecy. What is presidential spectacle? It is the utilization of modern media, especially television, to present the president in visible and highly dramatic actions designed to establish a favorable public identity. It is the presentation of the president in actions that minimize the potential for public interruption and treat citizens as passive spectators. Most important, it is the presentation of actions which are meaningful less for what they accomplish, in the sense of a substantive outcome, than for what they signify. Actions in a presidential spectacle serve as gestures rather than as means. Their power lies not in their efficacy, but in their impressiveness to the spectators.[10]

In a spectacle, the president becomes a larger-than-life character. He is made to appear exceptionally decisive, tough, brave, prudent, or the like. Whether he really possesses these qualities is another matter. What counts for the spectacle is that he appear to have strengths that ordinary citizens cannot imagine themselves as possessing. What counts for the spectacle is that he appear a confident and masterful leader before spectators whose passivity is the negation of any sense of mastery.

Unlike a "pure" spectacle—such as a concert as an example,—a presidential spectacle cannot be completely orchestrated in advance. Unanticipated events will occur; if the White House is skillful or lucky, it will capitalize on these events to embroider the spectacle. A presidential spectacle is also usually entangled with policy issues. Amid the actions that are designed as gestures will be activities whose importance is as genuine means to a policy end. The presidency is always more than a spectacle. But spectacle specialists are becoming a fixture on White House staffs, and the possibilities for staging spectacles through the media have been utilized with increasing sophistication. The gestures of the spectacle are becoming more prevalent, and are coming to dominate the public's perceptions of leadership in the White House.

Spectacle has been a feature of the presidency at least since the time of John F. Kennedy, the first "television" president. Some presidents have gotten little mileage out of it; the Ford and Carter presidencies provide instructive instances of spectacular misadventures. But the Reagan presidency, at least until the multiple missteps of its closing years, made maximum and generally effective use of the possibilities of spectacle. To illustrate presidential spectacle—and to indicate some of its distinctive dangers—I am thus going to turn to one of the Reagan administration's most extraordinary spectacles: Grenada.

In October 1983, the United States landed forces on the island of Grenada, justifying this action by the need to rescue American medical students and to move from power a violent Marxist clique. Grenada had a population of 100,000; its exports in 1981 totaled $19 million. U.S. invasion forces outnumbered the island's defenders approximately ten to one. This was hardly, in other words, an event with great military, political, or economic implications on a global scale. Nonetheless, President Reagan would proclaim in triumph: "Our days of weakness are over. Our military forces are back on their feet and standing tall."[11] Grenada's significance was as spectacle rather than as foreign policy. It was the spectacle of a president "standing tall."

The spectacle began with President Reagan on a weekend golfing vacation in Augusta, Georgia. His golfing was interrupted first by discussions of an invasion of Grenada and then by reports of the terrorist bombing of a Marine barracks in Beirut, Lebanon. Once the Grenada invasion took over the news from the tragedy in Beirut, the golf angle proved to be a colorful beginning for a spectacle. Thanks to the quick release of pictures taken by the White House photographer, the public could see a president swiftly shedding his normal relaxed approach and rising to meet a grave crisis. They could see photos of hurried conferences, in which a president in bathrobe and slippers was briefed by his foreign policy advisers, in which a secretary of state received the latest dispatch from Washington while still wearing his golf glove.

Photographs of the president as crisis decision maker, surrounded by his foreign policy team, were particularly dramatic because there were hardly any pictures from Grenada itself. The American press had been forbidden to accompany United States forces to the island. The Reagan administration's news management was infuriating to the press, but it served the needs of the spectacle. By shrouding what was actually happening on Grenada in secrecy and by controlling the flow of information to the American press and public, the administration was able to hide ugly or discrepant details and to cast the affair in terms of its own choosing. Reagan's Grenada spectacle would not have been helped by pictures of bloody corpses or wounded civilians. It would not have been as effective if critics in Congress had independent sources of information with which to raise questions about the Reagan administration's version of events.

The initial definition of the Grenada spectacle was established by President Reagan in his public announcement of the American action. The enemy was appropriately menacing; Reagan called them "a brutal group of leftist thugs . . ." The administration's objectives were impeccably moral— to rescue American medical students and to restore democratic government to the people of Grenada. Reagan's own action was an instance of clearly justifiable force; the United States, he said, "had no choice but to act strongly and decisively . . ."[12]

But the spectacle soon outdistanced this initial definition. Evacuation of the medical students from Grenada to the United States provided an unscripted scene that heightened the power of the spectacle. When some of the students kissed the airport tarmac, joyful at returning safely to American soil, the pictures on TV and in the newspapers were superior to anything the administration could have planned or hoped. They provided the Grenada spectacle with historical as well as emotional meaning. This had been another American hostage crisis—but where Jimmy Carter could not secure the freedom of captive Americans, Ronald Reagan had acted boldly and pulled off a heartwarming rescue.

Rescue of the students was dramatic enough, but the Reagan administration now played up an even more colorful theme. As President Reagan recounted the tale in his nationally televised address, "Grenada, we were told, was a friendly island paradise for tourism. Well, it wasn't. It was a Soviet-Cuban colony being readied as a major military bastion to export terror and undermine democracy. We got there just in time."[13] Grenada was becoming an ideal spectacle for Reagan. He had uncovered evil growing in a deceptive tropical landscape, and had eradicated it just before it flowered. He had come to the rescue not only on the students; the peoples of the Caribbean and throughout Latin America had also been save from impending subversion and terror by his daring action.

As Reagan's Grenada spectacle expanded in drama and heroics, the public rallied around the president. His poll ratings soared. Congressional critics, while skeptical of much of what the administration was saying, began to suppress nagging questions and leap onto the political bandwagon. A White House aide, quoted in *Newsweek,* gleefully made explicit the logic of presidential spectacle: "You can scream and shout and gnash your teeth all you want, but the folks out there like it. It was done right and done with dispatch." [14]

In its concluding gestures, the Grenada spectacle happily celebrated itself. President Reagan summoned the medical students to the White House and basked in their predictable cheers. The Pentagon chipped in its share of symbolic honors, handing out over 8,000 medals for the Grenada campaign—a figure that exceeded the number of American troops actually setting foot on the island. The spectacle was now too successful to be challenged by the discrepant details that continued to come to light. Grenada thus came to be, for most Americans, a highlight of Reagan's first presidential term and a vivid reassurance that "America is back." Insignificant in military or diplomatic terms, it was, as a spectacle, one of the central events of the Reagan presidency.

Secrecy and spectacle are two faces of the modern presidency. Secrecy conceals a good part of what presidents and their aides are doing; spectacle mystifies their activities. But as the story I have told about Grenada illustrates, these two faces are one. Secrecy serves spectacle; spectacle is undermined if the public becomes too knowing about what goes on behind the scenes of an administration. Information is frequently concealed not because of threats to national security, but because it might expose the hollowness of a president's spectacle gestures. And spectacle serves secrecy; the public is diverted by spectacular gestures and remains unaware of some of an administration's most fundamental—yet covert—objectives. Spectators are offered dramatizations of leadership that keep them in the dark about some of the most consequential acts by which leadership ought to be measured.

Secrecy and spectacle are intertwined in the modern presidency not only because each facilitates the other, but because they share a common core of doctrine. Seldom articulated, for obvious reasons, this doctrine posits the political incapacity of the American people. Presidents and their advisers, in this perspective, have a superior vantage point and superior knowledge for the making of important decisions. Public ignorance or emotions can hinder executive decision making—or can be enlisted in its support. Thus, the public must be shielded from events to which its reactions might prove squeamish or fearful, while provided with gestures that reassure and impress citizens through displays of presidential mastery. To put it bluntly, both secrecy and spectacle rest on an all too common White House disbelief in the assumptions and values of democratic political life.

The system of presidential secrecy and spectacle has been on the rise in recent years. Perhaps the most obvious danger it has posed is to presidential accountability. As Bernard Morris has emphasized, accountability means more than just responsibility. A president can take responsibility for the mistakes of his subordinates, and yet nothing is likely to happen to him. But accountability implies, in Morris' words, "some appropriate censure or penalty determined on constitutional, legal, institutional, or conventional grounds."[15] Secrecy and spectacle are both ways of circumventing accountability and disarming possible dissent. Both foster a contempt for the openness and honesty that are critical to any mode of democratic accountability. Both rest on the belief that a modern president should enjoy a sphere of unfettered will, and that he should not be held to account for what he does in that sphere.

Critics are customarily expected to propose remedies for the pathologies they have diagnosed. How, then, might we cope with the rise of secrecy and spectacle in the modern presidency? While institutional remedies developed in the face of the scandals of the 1970s, such as the establishment of congressional intelligence committees and new reporting requirements for the CIA, have made some modest improvements, the Iran-Contra affair shows how little headway we have made in controlling the excessive secrecy of the White House. Once the CIA was subjected to greater congressional oversight, the Reagan administration found new ways to circumvent such checks. The staff of the National Security Council was employed for covert activities, while CIA Director William Casey constructed an "off-the-shelf" covert capacity completely outside regular institutional boundaries. A new round of tightening congressional controls is certainly called for, but institutional constraints will not fundamentally tether the impulse to secrecy and the subterranean forms that secrecy can assume. Without rejecting institutional possibilities, then, I want to focus on a different approach—one which locates the essence of the problem not in procedures, but in the underlying worldview that has guided United States foreign policy for more than a generation.

The modern expansion of presidential secrecy needs to be seen as part and parcel of the rise of an American empire after World War II, and of an interventionist foreign policy that seeks to manipulate affairs in countries that pose little threat to American security, like Vietnam, Chile, and Nicaragua. I do not want to enter here into the complex debate over whether the forces behind the development of this empire are predominantly the economic imperatives of multinational corporations or the ideology and power instincts of a national security elite.[16] Suffice it to say that so long as the goals of American foreign policy remain imperial and the methods interventionist, so long as the attempt to determine the fate of other nations exceeds what can be justified even by the elastic claims of national interest and international benevolence, the sphere of secrecy and covert action will remain largely intact. If we wish to diminish the dangerous secrecy of the presidency, we need to confront the imperial mentality that demands such secrecy, a mentality that is fundamentally incompatible, as we should have recognized by now, with a constitutional republic. Without coming to terms with America's imperial identity and history, we will be unable to come to terms with the secrecy that distorts and corrupts the American presidency.

Combating spectacle is also more a matter of changed attitudes than changed institutions. Both the American media and the American public have to be willing to engage in greater reality testing. When viewing dramatic presidential actions, they need to ask: What does this event which we are witnessing really tell us about the president's purposes, his grasp of public affairs, his political skills? What does it really tell us about American power, productivity, or commitment to democratic values? When President Reagan told Americans that we were standing tall again because we had won a victory on Grenada, it would have made all the difference if a large number of Americans had laughed at such an absurd claim.

We are, to be sure, a long way from such reality testing. The press, fearful of losing access to White House sources, fearful even more of offending supporters of the president, is not soon going to measure presidential spectacles against the hard edge of reality. The public, tired of bad news and charmed by skillfully staged spectacles, may not want to listen to the press when it does interject more reality. The problem with reality testing is that it is painful. Still, we need to be reminded that a democratic society should prefer occasional pain to continual illusion.

Drastic reductions in presidential secrecy, and the replacement of spectacle with political dialogue, are necessary for democratic accountability. And they may, in the end, even be vital for presidential effectiveness.

Secrecy and spectacle mystify presidents too, nurturing cloistered fantasies on the one hand, manipulative stage illusions on the other. I suspect that this is one of the reasons why we have had a succession of presidents prone to disastrous miscalculations.

Secrecy and spectacle carry great appeal for presidents because both, singly and even more in tandem, promise short-term success. But if presidents were to reexamine the history of the office since World War II, they might wonder whether the costs might not be exceedingly high, not only for the American people but also for themselves. A president who had to face the American public more openly and more honestly might be helped to think and act more intelligently. In the end, the presidency needs democracy as much as does the citizenry the president is elected to serve. Secrecy and spectacle, nurtured by an imperial mentality, and productive of pervasive presidential falsity, are twin pathologies whose cure we need to seek, even as the particulars of their most recent disturbing manifestation begin to fade from view.

NOTES

1. Alexander Hamilton, James Madison, and John Jay, *The Federalist Papers,* edited by Clinton Rossiter (New York: New American Library, 1961), pp. 423–31.

2. John Tower, Edmund Muskie, and Brent Scowcroft, *The Tower Commission Report* (New York: Bantam Books, 1987), p. 344.

3. Quoted in Seymour M. Hersh, *The Price of Power: Kissinger in the Nixon White House* (New York: Summit Brooks, 1983), p. 265.

4. *The Tower Commission Report,* p. 468.

5. Ibid, p. 254.

6. Senate Select Committee to Study Governmental Operations with Respect to Intelligence Activities, *Alleged Assassination Plots Involving Foreign Leaders* (Washington, D.C.: U.S. Government Printing Office, 1975), p. 149.

7. Ibid.

8. Thomas Powers, *The Man Who Kept the Secrets: Richard Helms and the CIA* (New York: Pocket Books, 1981), p. 196.

9. On President Reagan's disengaged managerial style, see Lou Cannon, *Reagan* (New York: G. P. Putman's Sons, 1982), pp. 371–401 and Leslie H. Gelb, "The Mind of the President," *The New York Times Magazine,* October 6, 1985. On the amateurism of his NSC covert operatives, see *The Tower Commission Report.*

10. For a fuller treatment of spectacle than is possible here, see Bruce Miroff, "The Presidency and the Public: Leadership as Spectacle," in Michael Nelson, ed.,

The Presidency and the Political System, 2d ed. (Washington, D.C.: CQ Press, 1988), pp. 271–91.

11. Quoted in "Fare Well, Grenada," *Time,* December 26, 1983.

12. *New York Times,* October 26, 1983.

13. *New York Times,* October 28, 1983.

14. "We Will Not Be Intimidated," *Newsweek,* November 14, 1983.

15. Bernard Morris, "Presidential Accountability in Foreign Policy: Some Recurring Problems," in *Congress & the Presidency,* Volume 13, Number 2 (Autumn 1986), p. 159.

16. For an excellent account of the forces behind American imperial expansion, see Richard J. Barnet, *Roots of War: The Men and Institutions Behind U.S. Foreign Policy* (New York: Penguin Books, 1973).

INDEX

CASES CITED